Novel Arguments argues that innovative fiction—by which is meant writing that has been variously labeled as postmodern, metafictional, experimental—extends our ways of thinking about the world, rejecting the critical consensus that, under the rubrics of postmodernism and metafiction, homogenizes this fiction as autonomous and self-absorbed. Play, self-consciousness, and immanence—supposed symptoms of innovative fiction's autonomy—are here reconsidered as integral to its means of engagement. The book advances a concept of the "argument" of fiction as a construct wedding structure and content into a highly evolved and expressive form. The argument, not the content, is established as the site of a fiction's "aboutness," and thus the usual emphasis upon the generalities of innovative form is replaced by a concern for the logic of specific literary effects.

Close readings of five important innovative novels by Donald Barthelme, Ishmael Reed, Robert Coover, Walter Abish, and Kathy Acker show how they articulate matters of substance, social engagement, and ideological currency *by virtue* of the act of innovation. Walsh deftly argues for a new understanding of fictional cognition at the theoretical level, and, in an act of unmatched critical creativity, discards altogether the flattening totalities of received postmodern formulations.

T0370645

CAMBRIDGE STUDIES IN AMERICAN LITERATURE AND CULTURE 91

Novel Arguments

CAMBRIDGE STUDIES IN AMERICAN LITERATURE AND CULTURE

Other books in the series

Continued on pages following the Index

Novel Arguments

Reading Innovative American Fiction

RICHARD WALSH

Selwyn College, Cambridge

CAMBRIDGE
UNIVERSITY PRESS

CAMBRIDGE UNIVERSITY PRESS
Cambridge, New York, Melbourne, Madrid, Cape Town, Singapore, São Paulo, Delhi

Cambridge University Press
The Edinburgh Building, Cambridge CB2 8RU, UK

Published in the United States of America by Cambridge University Press, New York

www.cambridge.org
Information on this title: www.cambridge.org/9780521107037

First published 1995
This digitally printed version 2009

A catalogue record for this publication is available from the British Library

Library of Congress Cataloguing in Publication data
Walsh, Richard, 1964–
Novel arguments : reading innovative American fiction / Richard
Walsh.
p.   cm. – (Cambridge studies in American literature and
culture ; 91)
Includes bibliographical references and index.
ISBN 0–521–47145–1
1. American fiction—20th century—History and criticism.
2. Experimental fiction—United States—History and criticism.
3. Fiction—Technique. I. Title. II. Series.
PS374.E95W35   1995
813′.5409–dc20   94–36014
                                                              CIP

ISBN 978-0-521-47145-9 hardback
ISBN 978-0-521-10703-7 paperback

Contents

v

Preface

My interest in innovative fiction began with questions that must occur to everyone concerned with contemporary writing: What, at this stage in its history, can the novel do? What is it good for? I felt that the innovative fiction many American writers were producing from the mid-sixties to the mid-eighties offered an impressive range of answers to those questions. I wanted to think more carefully about what those novels were doing, and how they were doing it. It seemed appropriate to concentrate upon American writers, and not only because so much more innovative fiction came out of America than anywhere else. One of the reasons for that was the strong critical response to such writing in America, both positive and negative, which was itself related to the multiple social and cultural polarizations of the sixties. Yet in one respect this response was strangely uniform: the terms in which the enthusiasts of innovative writing sought to explain its innovation were almost indistinguishable from those in which its detractors sought to dismiss it. The growth and decline of interest in innovative fiction over this period seemed to reflect less a contest between views of innovation than a shifting evaluation of the same view. And since this view had to do with what innovative fiction was supposedly *not* doing (engaging with reality, being serious, even making sense), it gave little support to my own feeling that these writers had greatly enhanced the novel's means of doing these things. The case for innovative fiction as a valuable extension of our ways of thinking about the world was left largely unargued.

The book I have written attempts to make that argument, in general terms as well as by appeal to specific examples. In doing so, it pays close attention to the history of innovative fiction's reception in America, in the hope of releasing such fiction from a critical debate that has both sustained and discredited it. My intention has been to demonstrate and explain the nature of the misrepresentation, by advocates and opponents alike, that has consistently distracted criticism from an understanding of how innovative novels work. In chapter 1, I outline my own view of the means to such an understanding. I pursue that objective through the remaining five chapters, each of which is devoted to the interpretation of an exemplary work.

In the opening chapter I first identify the quality by which innovative fiction has been characterized throughout the period in question: its autonomy. Innovative novels, in various ways, have been taken to reject the fundamental concern with their social context that is an axiom for the realist novel. I show how this view gained currency from the misinterpretation of innovative writers' own comments, and from the critics' attempts to articulate the idea of autonomy in terms of emergent theoretical preoccupations. In particular, I consider the idea of autonomy in its three most common manifestations: as play, as self-consciousness and as immanence. The presence of these qualities in innovative fiction has been taken as a sign of its autonomy; my contention is that the apparent theoretical foundations for this, notably in structuralism and post-structuralism, have no such implications. Rather, a proper attention to the novels themselves reveals these same qualities in a new light, as integral to their means of engagement. In trying to specify what such a proper attention would be I have advanced a concept of the *argument* of fiction, as a means to displace criticism's too purely formal interest in innovation. I contrast the utility of this perspective on innovative fiction with the obfuscating results of criticism's obsession with postmodernism, and show the paradoxical self-referentiality of that discourse. It turns out that the self-referentiality of postmodernist criticism leaves it susceptible to the charge of autonomy in a way that, strikingly, does not apply to the use of metafictional self-reference by innovative writers.

One of the points about innovative fiction I want to insist upon is that, contrary to the impression of uniformity conveyed by much critical discussion, it has been remarkable for the diversity of its forms and the breadth of its preoccupations. My choice of writers and novels to discuss at length was influenced more by the wish to convey this diversity than by any misguided attempt to make them individually or collectively representative. The novels I have chosen span a period from 1975 to 1986—that is, from somewhere close to the peak of critical enthusiasm for innovative fiction to a point well down the decline in its status; or, from the urbane affability of Donald Barthelme, whose short stories were concurrently appearing in *The New Yorker*, to the subcultural intensity of Kathy Acker, writing and living abroad in London. My analysis of these novels seeks to demonstrate, by attending closely to the dynamics of form and substance, that they each achieve an effective articulation of their particular concerns *by virtue of their innovation*.

I have been using the phrase "innovative fiction" as if its meaning were self-evident, but since this is hardly the case I had better make some attempt to explain myself. In fact, "innovative fiction" is a quite deliberately vague label—it is intended to suggest the broadest of literary orientations, not a taxonomic category or a coherent aesthetic ideology, and certainly not a literary movement. It is an avoidance, for just this reason, of the several current terms that might be supposed to intersect with it. The two most prevalent alternatives, "postmodern fiction" and "metafiction," are inadequate to such a criterion, as well as being the subject of the more particular objections I raise in the opening chapter. I want a term that remains open to literary possibilities, rather than foreclosing them, and accordingly the only categorical definition of innovative fiction I can countenance is a negative one.

I would define innovative fiction, then, by distinguishing it from an equally capacious idea of realist fiction: it is not realist fiction in that it does not adhere to an aesthetic founded upon mimesis. I must immediately insist that this distinction is not antithetical, but a matter of degree. Any adequate concept of the realist tradition needs to recognize the extent to which mimetic criteria have varied throughout its history, and to register the equilibrium it has always negotiated between mimesis and the needs of narrative mediation. Also, such archetypally modernist forms as stream-of-consciousness writing

should be acknowledged as obedient to fundamentally mimetic imperatives. While innovative fictions cannot be understood in mimetic
terms, they are always mimetic to a certain degree. Indeed, no intelli-
gible narrative can manage entirely without mimesis, which is as
irreducible as its temporality and causality. The distinction rests, then,
upon innovative fiction's relative subordination of mimetic criteria,
and the logic of this subordination is that mimetic representation is
not conceived of as the primary vehicle of its engagement with the
world.

Mimetic principles dictate that realist fiction efface its formal attributes in the interests of immediacy, whereas innovative fiction is
characterized by the prominence and inventiveness of its forms. But
this does not equate innovation with constant formal novelty—such
a definition implies that unconventional forms are exhausted in the
use, and condemns innovative fiction to be eternally fugitive from
the formally *déjà fait*. It is common enough for hostile critics to
dismiss innovative fiction by discovering sources for its formal strategies, so revealing that it has "all been done before"—as if this proved
it in some way fraudulent. I think it a mistake to situate recent
innovative fiction in some anxious relation to the modernist avant-
garde, not because any particular idea of modernism is by now
defunct, but because the metaphor of the avant-garde is. Contemporary innovative writers do not present themselves as the van of formal
experimentation's triumphant march through literary history, because
such a linear progress no longer seems applicable to the art of fiction.
Instead, they are taking up the multitude of possibilities made available to that art by a less deferential attitude towards the aesthetic law
of mimesis.

Of course the idea of innovation does imply a "making new" of
some sort, but it is not of form in isolation, for form cannot be
dissociated from substance. Innovative fiction aims instead at a making new of fictional cognition—its originality lies in neither its form
nor its substance but in its *argument*. I offer this term as my best
attempt to name a concept central to the reading of innovative
fiction. The argument of a novel may be provisionally defined as the
formal articulation *of* its substance, the substance articulated *in* its
form. The word "argument" is current in literary terminology as the

abstract of a work: Milton offered such arguments before each book of *Paradise Lost,* as did Addison for Dryden's translation of the *Aeneid;* and Fielding, invoking the aura of epic origins, appropriated the practice to the contents pages of his novels. It would take no great neologistic enterprise to transfer this sense from the abstract to the work itself, and there already would be a term that to some extent subsumes the aspects of substance and form: "argument" as (an abstract of) both the significant content of the work in hand, and the narrative structure expressing that content. But I can appeal to the more general senses of the word in order to clarify and consolidate this double aspect. The *OED* offers several senses in which "argument" is to be understood as discursive matter of a particular sort; but also the sense in which it indicates the form of a discourse, as "a connected series of statements."[1] "Argument," then, can mean the *structure* of proof, or its *material.* A more general formulation of these two possible applications of the word gives me the duality of reference—to the form of the referent and to its substance—that I need. The distinction can be seen in common usage: "the argument is about . . ." takes the form as given, and proceeds to the particulars of substance; but "the argument is that . . ." assumes the substance, and seeks to elucidate the form of the reasoning. The term "argument," then, contains both formal and substantial senses in exactly the right relation, that of complementary *aspects* of the same phenomenon.

Defined in this way, the argument of a novel can be understood as the sum of its effects. It is not to be confined to the rational and assertive, but includes the imaginary, the interrogative, the aesthetic and especially the emotional qualities of the novel. By paying attention to the argument of fiction, I have tried to show how to avoid treating the form of innovative fiction as the whole of its rationale. Criticism that falls into this trap, whether it is with enthusiasm or distaste, robs fiction of its specificity and finally renders it trivial. As I hope my discussion of these novels will show, it is far from that.

Acknowledgments

This book began as a doctoral thesis, under the supervision of Tony Tanner; my thanks go first of all to him, for the measure of his criticism and for his generous advocacy of my work ever since. I would also like to thank John Harvey, Rod Mengham, Ian Bell and Jean Chothia, who have all read and commented upon this work at various stages, and been active in their support. My editors at Cambridge University Press, Vicki Cooper in Cambridge and Susan Chang and Stephanie Doyle in New York, have been industrious in my interest. I am grateful to Selwyn College, Cambridge, for the Keasbey Research Fellowship in American Studies during which this project was completed.

Several chapters of this book have previously appeared, in earlier and shorter form, in the following volumes: chapter 6 in *Critique*, 32 (1991); chapter 2 in *Critical Essays on Donald Barthelme*, ed. Richard F. Patteson (New York: G.K. Hall, 1992); chapter 3 in *Journal of American Studies*, 27 (1993); and chapter 4 in *Studies in the Novel*, 25 (1993).

Chapter 1

The Idea of Innovative Fiction

In 1985, the *Mississippi Review* devoted a special issue to the new fiction of the moment, by which was intended the work of writers like Raymond Carver, Ann Beattie, Frederick Barthelme and Joan Didion. Editor Kim Herzinger, attempting to name the phenomenon, considered the currency of such labels as "Dirty Realism," "New Realism," "Pop Realism," "TV Fiction," "Neo-Domestic Neo-Realism" and "Post-Alcoholic Blue-Collar Minimalist Hyperrealism," but settled upon "Minimalist Fiction."[1] This literary christening was significant less in itself than in terms of its reaction against what had gone before: it was the logical culmination of a process by which the proliferation of innovative fictions in America since the sixties had come to be caricatured as the products of an aesthetic decadence. One of the writers associated with that decadence, John Barth, characterized the ensuing minimalist impulse as a recurrent feature of human affairs, a revolt initiated by "the feeling that the language (or whatever) has for whatever reasons become excessive, cluttered, corrupted, fancy, false. It is the Puritan's reaction against baroque Catholicism; it is Thoreau's putting behind him even the meager comforts of the village of Concord."[2] In doing so he himself accepted the fundamental dichotomy underlying the contemporary appeal of minimalism: that fiction also tended towards the functional or the merely ornamental, according to the modesty or exuberance of its form. Such a model credited "minimalist fiction" with initiating, after a period of fictional self-absorption and frivolity, a salutary revival of realism and a new straightforward engagement with the

1

material of contemporary reality. One might argue that this fiction was doing something rather smaller than that, in terms of both the "realities" it sought to engage and the means by which it did so. In fact if we accept for a moment the critical archetype of this fiction—its blue collar, midwestern, quotidian subject matter; its flat, spare style, reticent about all but the surface of events, abstaining from metaphor in its desire to impose upon language a purely literal narrative function—it seems to be defined much less by an ideal of direct engagement with reality than by the repression of everything that might bring that ideal into question.

Realism need not be invoked in such crude terms: the crudity in this case merely reflected the crudity of the model of innovative fiction against which it was set. My concern here is to revise that model, and a necessary first step is to refuse the terms of the opposition. Realist fictions may be understood broadly as those that undertake, through whatever choice of formal strategies, to engage with the world primarily through *mimesis*. It is a condition of this mode of engagement that mimesis is recognized as such, and by various means (explicitly and implicitly) realism acknowledges and frames its means of representation. Innovative fictions are by no means antithetical in their assumptions; they too are aimed at engagement with the world. What they reject, to different degrees, is the centrality of mimesis as a mode of engagement. This is not a negative or restrictive strategy: the chief merit innovative fictions share is their capacity to extend the possibilities of fictional engagement *beyond* mimesis.

This is not the conventional view of innovative fiction. Such fiction began to appear with increasing frequency during the sixties, and at first it *was* assumed that its formal innovation was an attempt to engage the vital concerns of the times—not a frivolous disregard for them.[3] But during the seventies a critical consensus began to emerge, not only that innovative fiction was turning *away* from reality, but that this was in fact its defining quality. How? The root causes of such a reversal are accessible only to speculation, but it is possible to trace the development of the notion through a collaborative series of misinterpretations and misrepresentations of the fiction itself, of the statements of its practitioners and of its theoretical context; and so, I hope, to make space for an alternative history of this fiction as consistently and valuably engaged.

VERSIONS OF AUTONOMY

An initial problem was that innovative fictions attracted critical attention for their formal interest, regardless of the uses to which those formal strategies were put. Soon the dominance of questions of form in the criticism led to the assumption that all other issues were subordinate in the fiction itself. Formal interest alone was established as the yardstick of such writing, and innovative fiction inevitably began to be regarded as autonomous and autotelic, a law unto itself and an end in itself.

The sources of this critical misrepresentation of innovative fiction lie close to several of its advocates and mediators, whose (often misappropriated) observations lent it cumulative weight. For example, John Barth's surprisingly influential essay "The Literature of Exhaustion" was certainly a formative text. It was generally understood to have pronounced the finitude of the possible forms by which fiction may map reality; these forms having been exhausted, all that remained to the writer was to transcend his redundancy and take it for his subject matter. Barth was not wholly innocent of such a thesis; but in his defence, this was a misreading of the essay. His argument was not universal, but referred only to "the used-upness of certain forms or exhaustion of certain possibilities."[4] He was concerned throughout to distinguish between "the *fact* of aesthetic ultimacies and their artistic *use*," and his praise for Borges was couched in terms of his ability to go beyond the realization of an exhausted form: "His artistic victory, if you like, is that he confronts an intellectual dead end and employs it against itself to accomplish new human work."[5] Barth's argument was for the capability of the metafictional, self-cancelling text to generate, paradoxically, a reinvigorated fictional perspective that escaped the literary solipsism of its origins. For his readers, though, it was the giddy void of that solipsism that overwhelmed the imagination.

In a larger context, Susan Sontag's "Against Interpretation" contributed significantly to the emergence of the necessary critical disposition. In that essay she denigrated interpretation in favour of "experiencing the luminousness of the thing in itself," and famously concluded, "In place of a hermeneutics we need an erotics of art."[6] The apotheosis of this tendency was that celebration of form as an autonomous source of aesthetic pleasure described by Sontag in "Notes on Camp." Although she clearly declared her own ambivalence towards the camp sensibility, its essential features—the exclusive concentration upon questions of style, the uncritical generosity towards all details of argument, import or intent and the consequent passive relation towards contemporary consumer culture—delineated in caricature the emphases and inadequacies of an emerging trend in the criticism of innovative fiction.

Sontag's simultaneous distance from and promotion of this sensibility was characteristic of the advocates of innovative fiction in the sixties. The continuing dominance of a conservative aesthetic in academic and publishing circles often goaded these advocates into a certain stridency, into promoting theoretical positions they did not hold or would not have themselves accepted without qualification. William Gass was one such whose influence upon contemporary innovative fiction and criticism was considerable. Gass was always embattled against the non-aesthetic tradition of those philosopher-critics who "continue to interpret novels as if they were philosophies themselves . . . they have predictably looked for content, not form; they have regarded fictions as ways of viewing reality and not as additions to it."[7] Standing against such a view of fiction, he often seemed to simply reverse these polarities, to concentrate exclusively upon form, to regard fictions as additions to reality without acknowledging that this was not inconsistent with their offering certain modes of viewing the same. "There are no descriptions in fiction, there are only constructions."[8] This statement appears flatly to deny fictional representation in favour of autonomous linguistic structure, and Gass's position was often taken as such. But the distinction was between fictional processes, not products: Gass was insisting that a fictional world is not created through a word-by-word correspondence to reality (or some perception of it) but by the qualifications and elaborations of words in relation to each other. His argument was with the concept of fiction as primarily a mode of *mimesis,* for which he substitutes one of fiction as linguistic structure. But in asserting the primacy of the signifier Gass neglected and often appeared to deny its *signification,* and so nourished a delusory concept of the autonomy of the literary object amongst his sympathizers and offered an easy target for his detractors. The actual position Gass and others wished to assert regarding fiction was necessarily misrepresented by this oppositional stance, because the argument involved a double movement: first an insistence upon the medium of language, then a measured recognition of its signifying function that was always underplayed, because the battle lines of the debate gave it the appearance of a concession.

As critics became receptive to the idea of literary autonomy they began to look for, and find, evidence of it in contemporary fiction. In particular, it seemed possible to identify three qualities of this fiction that demonstrated its autonomy: play, self-consciousness and immanence. The model of fiction as play became a commonplace of 1970s' criticism. Philip Stevick, in a 1974 essay that explored "Metaphors for the Novel," concluded that "the novel is a game. If we try to hold in the mind some representative recent fiction—*City Life, Breakfast of Champions, The Blood Oranges, Gravity's Rainbow*—what seems to unite them is an autotelic, nonreferential quality in which the value of the fiction inheres in its invention, its wit and intricacy of texture, its appeal as a made thing, obedient to no laws but its own."[9] Stevick's intention was to affirm the fiction he described, yet he explicitly stated the antipathy of his version of fictional play to the expression of any response to reality: "Either fiction is a game or it is an expressive vehicle—or so it would seem—not both. . . . there does seem to be a special exclusivity between playing and finding ways of expressing our deepest feelings about the world."[10] Accordingly, he ended by affirming the dominance of play-oriented qualities in the new fiction while simultaneously locating its ultimate value in the very function against which they were seen to operate: "When it succeeds, it is as re-creative, clever and autotelic as it can be while still preserving its expressive function."[11] The vulnerability of this affirmation is apparent in the similar concept of play advanced by

Leslie Fiedler, who represented it as a rejection of modernist seriousness and the pretensions of high art, part of the process by which
high and popular culture were to be conflated.[12] As with Stevick,
play was simple antiseriousness, but here its hegemony implied a flat
refusal of any engagement whatever. I would argue that the playfulness of many innovative fictions should be understood as an important means, entirely consistent with an attitude of serious engagement. Jean Piaget's model of play would have been better: play as
inquiry or exploration without a preemptive agenda; play as engagement without presupposition. But the critical enthusiasts of play
chose to affirm it in autonomous terms—and so exposed innovative
fiction to charges of triviality. And indeed, it is difficult to see how
such a view of fiction could have held any interest for critics: if it did,
it may paradoxically have been due to the aura of seriousness that
the concept of play acquired from structuralist and post-structuralist
theory.

The significance of play in this context derives in the first instance
from the Saussurian concept of meaning as the product of relations
within the structure of language rather than of correspondence *between*
language and reality. The "play of the signifier" is a result of this
model of language, because meaning ceases to be something fixed in
the individual sign, and becomes instead an unstable effect of the
multiple differences *between* signs. The distinction between the concept of play that inhered in the structuralist model and its universal-
ized post-structuralist version was elaborated by Jacques Derrida, in a
critique of structuralism via Lévi-Strauss; its significance was enhanced by the fact that it remained for some time the only translated
text by which Derrida was known in America. He showed how
structuralism depended upon a concept of centre or origin that limited the play of the structure, but was itself immune to this play:
"The concept of a centered structure is in fact the concept of a play
based on a fundamental ground, a play constituted on the basis of a
fundamental immobility and a reassuring certitude, which in itself is
beyond the reach of play. . . . Thus it has always been thought that
the center, which is by definition unique, constituted that very thing
within a structure which while governing the structure, escapes struc-
turality."[13] In the face of this contradiction, Derrida perceived two

possibilities, which for many critics seemed to provide a framework for distinguishing between realist fiction and innovative fiction in terms of limited and free play: "There are thus two interpretations of interpretation, of structure, of sign, of play. The one seeks to decipher, dreams of deciphering a truth or an origin which escapes play and the order of the sign, and which lives the necessity of interpretation as an exile. The other, which is no longer turned toward the origin, affirms play and tries to pass beyond man and humanism. . . ."[14] Derrida was widely taken to be the apostle of the latter creed, and therefore the authority to which a manifesto for innovative fiction could appeal. In fact he declared that, "For my part, although these two interpretations must acknowledge and accentuate their difference and define their irreducibility, I do not believe that today there is any question of *choosing*."[15] But in any case, neither one implied a literary program—they were interpretations of *interpretation*, two modes of approaching the play inherent in any discourse, one of which posited a lost origin that the other discarded, but neither of which allowed that this state of affairs was affected by the specific practices or intentions of a particular text. The association between innovative fiction and autonomous play was a critical decision, not a literary one.

Self-consciousness, the second of the critics' symptoms of fiction's autonomy, is a term by which I mean to designate the broadest spectrum of attributes that draw attention to, or show awareness of, the medium of fiction—its language, its form or its fictionality. It includes, but is not limited to, the special case of self-*reference* which I take to be the domain of metafiction, and which needs to be discussed in its own right. The equivalence of these two terms was assumed by many critics, and self-consciousness was stigmatized accordingly, as the replacement of fiction's attention to the world by its attention to itself. Yet this was not the case, even for such ardent advocates of the medium as William Gass. He put it best in a 1982 essay, "Representation and the War for Reality"—its title indicative of the escalation of critical hostilities by this date. Here he clearly characterized his emphasis upon the sign as essential to an engaged concept of fiction: "A novel is a mind aware of a world," he declared, but "if the inscription is skimped, *what* is read?"[16] His commitment to the sign was justified by an emphasis upon its *mediating* function, its central importance as the site of the mind's attention to reality: "Although, without rules of representation, there can be no correlation between matter and mind, system of data; nevertheless, without notation, these two can not be brought together in the same place. It, not the pineal, is the true Cartesian gland."[17]

Gass's version of self-consciousness centred upon the persistence of the literary sign as sign, and as such always significant. A rather different model of self-consciousness was promoted by Ronald Sukenick, one of the leading theoretical apologists of the Fiction Collective. His concern was less with the material of fiction than the process; but he was equally far from advocating self-consciousness as a withdrawal from reality. Instead he argued that fiction, by promoting an awareness of the contingency of its narrative forms in their formulation, could foster a more rigorous attention not to the medium ultimately, but to the empirical world beyond: "Such fictive truth simultaneously proposes and cancels itself, not to deny the autonomous reality of the world, but to salvage it from the formulations of language. The provisional nature of fictive language allows it both its imaginative freedom and its claim to truth. . . . affirmation of the medium has provided an authority for the way out of a modernist hermeticism back into an investigation of common experience."[18] For Sukenick that provisional authority lay in the self-declaration of the medium as a barrier to the experience it enunciates, a strong contrast with its celebration as the site of meaning in Gass; but both forms of self-consciousness were offered as means of engagement.

This logic of self-consciousness, that attention to the medium always leads back to an awareness of its mediation, had already been worked through in the essays of Roland Barthes—who, like Derrida, was nonetheless widely suspected of undermining the foundations of fiction's capacity to mean in the world. In "To Write: An Intransitive Verb?"—a paper delivered at the very symposium that introduced Derrida to the American academy—Barthes applauded the increased self-consciousness of recent fiction. Although he was doubtless alluding to the *nouveau roman,* his description was couched in terms easily appropriated to the defence of much American innovative fiction:

modern literature is trying, through various experiments, to establish a new status in writing for the agent of writing. The meaning
or the goal of this effort is to substitute the instance of discourse
for the instance of reality (or of the referent), which has been, and
still is, a mythical "alibi" dominating the idea of literature. The
field of the writer is nothing but writing itself, not as the pure
"form" conceived of by an aesthetic of art for art's sake, but, much
more radically, as the only area [*espace*] for the one who writes.[19]

This fits well with the enterprises of many American innovators, but
it is certainly *not* a version of autonomous fiction. It engages the
world precisely by refusing the "alibi" of reference by which realism
effaces the "instance of discourse." The point is that fiction never
presents an immediate reality, but only the discourses within which it
is inscribed. Self-effacing mimetic representation is itself a product of
fiction's indexing of other discourses, not a direct window upon the
world. Barthes rejected the idea of intransitive writing expressed in
his title in favour of a model based on the linguistic category of *voice*.
The verb *to write* is not to be understood in the active (subject/
author centred), nor in the passive (object/referent centred) but in
the middle voice: "In the case of the middle voice . . . the subject
affirms himself in acting, he always remains inside the action, even if
an object is involved. The middle voice does not, therefore, exclude
transitivity. Thus defined, the middle voice corresponds exactly to
the state of the verb *to write:* today to write is to make oneself the
center of the action of speech [*parole*]; it is to effect writing in being
affected oneself; it is to leave the writer [*scripteur*] inside the writing,
not as a psychological subject . . . but as the agent of the action."[20]

So, in "Authors and Writers," Barthes made a hypothetical distinction between the author [*écrivain*], who focusses upon language, and
the writer [*écrivant*], who disregards the medium of language and
attempts to deal directly with the world. But he went on to argue
that the author's self-consciousness was not an aesthetic solipsism, but
rather a concentration upon language that leads inexorably *back* to the
world: "by enclosing himself in the *how to write,* the author ultimately
discovers the open question par excellence: why the world? What is
the meaning of things? In short, it is precisely when the author's

work becomes its own end that it regains a mediating character: the author conceives of literature as an end, the world restores it to him as a means: and it is in this perpetual inconclusiveness, that the author rediscovers the world, an alien world moreover, since literature represents it as a question—never, finally, as an answer."[21] It is in language, not brute reality, that meaning is to be found; so that by attending to language the author does not neglect the question of engagement, but opens it—it is exactly this attention to the medium that certifies literature's mediation. Which is to say that the heightened self-consciousness of much innovative fiction, while it disregards the imperatives of realism, does not at all neglect to interrogate the real.

The third quality by which critics characterized the supposed autonomy of innovative fiction has been variously termed, but it involves the collapse of the distinction between representation and the real, or the perceived immanence of the latter in the former. This is not self-conscious attention to the language of fiction *as medium,* for it can no longer be said to mediate anything. Instead, linguistic representation becomes meaningless and fiction is to be appreciated as a mute object.

The perverse appeal of this concept to some critical enthusiasts of innovative fiction is best illuminated by the work of Jerome Klinkowitz, who modelled the immanence of fiction by an analogy with the other arts. Innovative writers, he argued, "establish their books not just as linguistic games but as imaginatively created objects in the world, where fiction can have the same appreciated existence as painting, sculpture, music, or any of the arts."[22] The equation between fiction and painting allowed him to confuse literary *meaning* with the *subject* of painting, signification with mimesis, and so to defend "disruptive" fiction as the equivalent of Abstract Expressionism. In his later criticism he extended this logic to "experimental realism," conceived of as analogous to superrealism in painting. In this fiction, exemplified by Walter Abish, Stephen Dixon, Kenneth Gangemi and Leonard Michaels, Klinkowitz argued for the possibility of linguistic "self-apparency," in which the reader's attention is detained on the linguistic surface of the text, within a context of broadly realist narration, such that any apparent claim to represent reality is cancelled. Here representation is indulged precisely *because* it is meaningless: according to Klinkowitz, "To practise writing is not to parody signifying, it is to destroy the very practice of signifying itself. Materiality of text is the product of this destruction, and makes reading an attractive and rewarding activity."[23] It's not entirely clear how: in affirming the materiality of the text *at the expense of* its signifying capacity, Klinkowitz conceded freely to the charge of disengagement levelled at innovative fiction and so, effectively, to the charge of its triviality.

Undeniably, concepts of immanence held a certain interest for a number of innovative novelists: such a disposition was notably present in the critical statements of Ronald Sukenick and Raymond Federman. But despite Klinkowitz's interpretation, the intention even here was to make immanence serve the ends of engagement. Sukenick proposed a new opacity in fiction, which was to be experienced "in and for itself. It is opaque the way that abstract painting is opaque in that it cannot be explained as representing some other kind of experience. You cannot look through it to reality—it is the reality in question and if you don't see it you don't see anything at all."[24] Federman also insisted that fiction could no longer be "a representation of reality, or an imitation, or even a recreation of reality; it can only be A REALITY. . . ."[25] But the point of this attempt to collapse the dichotomy between language and reality, leaving fiction as pure event, was not to escape reality, but language: the idea was to exploit the opportunity for the immediate presentation of experience that immanence appeared to offer. Against the model of fiction that aspired to a faithful imitation of the nature of reality, Sukenick wished to assert a "poetic truth" of fiction: "This kind of 'truth' does not depend on accurate description of reality but rather itself generates what we call reality, reordering our perceptions and sustaining a vital connection with the world, and may be considered on a parity with truth generated in other disciplines that extend, reorder, and vitalize the human domain. It works against schizoid withdrawal into abstraction or solipsism, and at the same time works against entrapment in its own tautologies by constantly dissolving them into experience."[26]

At stake in this contested concept is the possibility, and desirability, of fiction retaining its capacity as critique, rather than mere symptom, of the culture in which it is produced. When the material of knowledge and the function of knowing are reduced to the same plane, discourse loses the exteriority to its subject that makes an oppositional literature possible. Many critics felt that if innovative fiction was flirting with immanence, it should be repudiated in defence of the values of social and moral engagement. John Gardner's insistence in *On Moral Fiction* that the true vocation of fiction was an honest imaginative engagement with reality through a seamless medium, and Gerald Graff's arguments against the effacement of reality he found central to postmodernism in *Literature Against Itself,* are only the most prominent of such responses. Very different manifestations of the same impulse are found in John Aldridge's dismissive evaluation of innovative fiction according to conservative literary criteria in *The American Novel and the Way We Live Now,* and in Charles Newman's impatience with its supposed perpetuation of a redundant project to undermine the concept of objective reality in *The Post-Modern Aura,* where innovative fiction is merely the product of a culture understood in terms of the metaphor of inflationary economics.[27]

Gerald Graff identified innovative writers' scepticism about representation and the hermeneutic authority by which it may be grounded as itself symptomatic. He argued that the sort of authoritative value system that an artist can define him- or herself against by mere subversion was no longer present in contemporary consumer society. The artist's alienated stance had ceased to represent a critical relation to society, but become normative, and so paradoxically assimilated: in contemporary America, "consumer society not only popularizes ideologies of alienation, to an increasing extent it invests its capital in them."[28] In order to maintain an oppositional stance, Graff concluded, the writer must *lay claim* to authority rather than subverting it. Yet he failed to provide the grounds for such authority. He acknowledged that the "deterioration of language" that was central to his diagnosis implied a delegitimation of the discourse of ideological opposition as well as of society's assimilated discourses, but then proposed a way out that merely sidestepped the problem: "One way of avoiding this dead end is to make the deterioration of language one of the objects of the fictional criticism of society, to infuse it into the typology of character and setting. The corruption of language then ceases to be merely an occasion for novelistic introversion or wordplay but becomes seen as a social fact, spreading into personal and collective relations."[29] Lest this project should seem too close to the interrogations of language being undertaken by some of the very writers he was opposing, Graff was careful to insist upon the author's transcendent position in relation to a degenerate language contained within "the typology of character and setting." This left the author's own language unexamined, granting it authoritative status as the delineator of "social fact." His confident exemption of the author indicated that Graff was thinking of a lesser order of linguistic degeneration than some of the writers he criticized. In fact, if we are to take seriously the theorist who has developed the concept of immanence most fully, then it was not that innovative fiction had irresponsibly relinquished its critical distance; rather, the distinction between critique and symptom itself had become universally invalid.

That theorist is Jean Baudrillard, whose arguments for the immanence of media in contemporary culture were anchored in a post-Marxist frame of reference strongly influenced by Marshall McLuhan: "*the medium is the message* signifies not only the end of the message, but also the end of the medium. There are no longer media in the literal sense of the term (I am talking above all about the electronic mass media)—that is to say, a power mediating between one reality and another, between one state of the real and another—neither in content nor in form."[30] Under such circumstances, he argued, the images, representations and cultural products in which media deal had become in themselves part of the economic sphere: the distinction between base and superstructure had collapsed. Consequently, there had arisen a "political economy of the sign," in which its referential function had become an irrelevance. These considerations drove Baudrillard's own discourse towards an extreme and ultimately nihilist position. He insisted that his argument, being itself implicated in the cultural logic it described, was denied any status as a critique; but he also insisted that "the system itself is . . . nihilist, in the sense that it has the power to reverse everything in indifferentiation, including that which denies it."[31] For Baudrillard too, then, the immanence of media obliterated the distinction between cultural critique and cultural symptom. But this diagnosis did not rely upon the evidence of innovative fiction: in fact, he argued that its cultural manifestations did not enact an absence of reference, but actually *simulated* reference. Simulation is the manufacture of the "hyperreal," substituting for and masking a lost reality—ultimately, a condition in which the sign's referential charade "bears no relation to any reality whatsoever: it is its own pure simulacrum."[32]

Baudrillard's argument is typical of postmodern theoretical discourse in situating itself simultaneously within and outside its own frame of reference. Accordingly, it has a dense validity within the terms of its own premises, yet its engagement with actual cultural conditions is strictly undecidable. But if the concept of immanence implies this argument, the positions in the debate on innovative fiction are effectively reversed. John Gardner's concept of "moral fiction," for example, postulated a text that enabled the reader to enter a "vivid and continuous dream, living a virtual life, making moral judgements in a virtual state" and to be led through this virtual world to whatever affirmation the writer had found able to endure fictive exploration.[33] The process by which the writer reached this affirmation was given great emphasis by Gardner: to be truly moral it had to be earned by a continuous testing and revision of the emerging narrative against a standard of truth to life. The status of this standard of course begged the whole question, but what was peculiar about the form advocated by Gardner was the disparity between the writer's experience of it and the reader's. If the morality of this fiction was so crucially located in the process of its composition, that process was largely lost on the reader. Gardner's solution was, quite explicitly, for the fiction to provide a simulacrum of that process: "In this process I describe, the reader is at a disadvantage in that what he has before him is not all the possibilities entertained by the writer and recognized as wrong but only the story the writer eventually came to see as inevitable and right. But the good writer provides his reader, consciously and to some extent mechanically, with a dramatic equivalent of the intellectual process he himself went through. That equivalent is suspense."[34] But suspense is end-directed in a way the moral explorations of the writer are not: for all of Gardner's insistence upon the reader's active role, his model of fiction presented reading as a passive, simulated moral engagement. By comparison, Ronald Sukenick's model of the author's self-consciousness about the process of writing, which in this case could actually be seen to be generating the fiction, fares very favourably as a strategy against the simulated "hyperreality" of immanent media.

Play, self-consciousness, immanence: the tendency of critics to seize upon such concepts as indicators of the autonomy of innovative fiction suggests that the underlying difficulty lay in their sense that in thus presenting itself—as narrative, as fiction, as language—such fiction inverted the relation of form and content upon which their notion of engagement depended.

THE ARGUMENT OF FICTION

The dichotomy of form and content in critical thinking has proved indurate, despite the fact that its theoretical invalidity is almost universally acknowledged. The inevitable consequence of this conceptual framework—that realism was equated with the primacy of content, and innovation with the primacy of form—dictated the terms in which innovative fiction was applauded *and* reviled throughout the seventies. In the eighties several critics responded to this blunt opposition by advocating a synthesis in which the values of both realist and innovative fictions might be incorporated into a single framework. John Barth, in "The Literature of Replenishment," was a case in point: "A worthy program for postmodernist fiction, I believe, is the synthesis or transcension of these antitheses. . . . The ideal postmodernist novel will some how rise above the quarrel between realism and irrealism, formalism and 'contentism,' pure and committed literature, coterie fiction and junk fiction."[35] Charles Newman formulated essentially the same program, with less confidence in the ability of the "postmodernist novel" to realize it, in *The Post-Modern Aura:* "If the Post-Modern were capable of setting itself an obvious task, it would be the recombinancy of 19th century emotional generosity with the technical virtuosity of the 20th."[36] But in advancing such arguments, both writers acquiesced in the polarities that defined the debate, the antithesis between formalist purity, disengagement, technical aridity, and realist transparency, responsibility, humanity—

an antithesis justified by neither example nor theory. Realism is itself a formal framework, or rather a repertoire of formal frameworks, the conventions of which have been broadly assimilated as modes of textual cognition. Conversely, and more importantly for the argument in hand, formalism (in literature) is always the imposition of narrative or aesthetic structure upon language, and therefore a mode of signification of *something:* that much at least is consequent upon the referentiality of the medium.

Other critical syntheses of the dualism of innovation and realism proceeded from a more empirical base, professing to have identified the transcendent form in some contemporary fiction, which for Jerome Klinkowitz was "experimental realism," and for Alan Wilde was "midfiction." Klinkowitz's attempt to affirm both form and content was, as I have already suggested, a cosmetic revamping of autonomous formalism and simply resulted in two unresolved and incompatible concepts of the fiction it described. According to one concept, the value of fiction lay on the linguistic surface: "The joy of self-apparent signs is their lack of hierarchy and informed meaning, which allows the reader to experience them with a full sense of their being."[37] According to the other, value was located precisely in the passage *through* fiction to reality: "We know reality only through our fictions, which is the task experimental realism takes upon itself anew."[38] The concept of experimental realism was a simple yoking of the formalist and realist concepts of fiction, not their synthesis.

Alan Wilde's concept of "midfiction" was based on a more strictly synthetic logic, being "the kind of fiction which rejects equally the oppositional extremes of realism on the one hand and a world-denying reflexivity on the other."[39] He invoked Donald Barthelme, Thomas Pynchon, Stanley Elkin, Max Apple, Thomas Berger and Grace Paley as the exponents of a "referential but non-mimetic literature."[40] This formulation recognized that the criteria for engagement with reality might be distinguished from the criteria for realism—an important discovery; but Wilde's designation of this middle ground as "referential" was actually more restrictive than it seemed. For Wilde the phrase implied all the qualities of realism save verisimilitude: the archetype of such a literature would be the parable, "which, like midfiction (and unlike metafiction) founds itself on the interaction of generally plausible characters and more or less consequent, if often unexpected, events in a narrative whose setting is deliberately and determinedly concrete, sensuous, and ordinary. . . ."[41] Midfiction, then, constructed parallel worlds with only a contingent relation to reality, but which remained, on their own terms, broadly obedient to realist conventions. For Wilde, these parallel worlds provided a field in which the cognitive understanding of author or reader was exercised in ways familiar enough to evoke the operation of the same processes in the real world: midfiction invited us "to perceive, obliquely and ironically, the moral perplexities of inhabiting a world that is itself, as 'text,' ontologically contingent and problematic."[42] He thus equated fiction and reality as "text," while simultaneously effacing the textuality of fiction. In spite of his claim to the middle ground between innovation and realism, his orientation was strongly towards a figurative form of the latter. Innovation was reduced to the mere refusal of literal realism, and made no further contribution to either his concept of midfiction or his interpretation of individual texts.

These attempts to vindicate certain texts or authors by appeal to a synthetic logic should be rejected, above all, because they tax fiction with resolving—and sanctioning—the incoherences of critical terminology. A more careful consideration of the confused concepts of form and content would have released innovative fiction from the assumption that its accommodation to realism is a condition of its engagement. In the first place, "content" is in itself a misleading term: not only because it characterizes form as a container, and so implicitly contradicts all declarations of the inseparability of the two; but also because it is too readily equated, in its own right, with the ultimate "aboutness" of a text. A better distinction would be between form and substance, or matter: in such terms unity is an axiom established since Aristotle, and it is universal, not evaluative. This puts Coleridge's distinction between "mechanic" and "organic" form in context, the superior unity attributed to the latter being a secondary phenomenon related to a particular concept of artistic integrity, and referring less to the product than the process of literature. "The" form of a literary text, if it is possible to conceive of such a thing except in terms of genre, is always a cumulation of formal decisions, principles of organization applied to different orders of substance. Writing fiction is the forming of substances to signify a third thing, which may itself be regarded as substance to be formed. Words themselves are already significant forms when the writer comes upon them, and it is these significations that are organized to generate the functional units of narrative (characters or concepts, actions or propositions) that are themselves orchestrated to produce higher-order phenomena (plots and themes) that are also susceptible to the shaping process. The ultimate product, a fiction, is a complex, stratified object: its substance, or what is commonly called its content, is achieved in a particular form such that a final third thing is evoked. This I am calling, for want of a better word, the *argument* of the fiction, which I take to have aesthetic and affective, as well as logical attributes. The argument, not the content, is the site of a fiction's aboutness, and it is articulated in the *process* of informing that content. Because to ask what a fiction is *about* is to ask what it is *doing:* its argument is not what is written, but what is worked through.

With this in mind, it is possible to see that innovation, far from being a refusal of engagement, is an attempt to extend fiction's capacity for thinking about the world. The comments of innovative novelists themselves, throughout the sixties and seventies, repeatedly testified that their unfamiliar methods were conceived of as precisely a means by which to grapple with the complexity of contemporary reality, to bring into consciousness those of its facets that conventional perceptions excluded. John Hawkes notoriously declared his enabling premises as a writer to have been that "the true enemies of the novel were plot, character, setting and theme."[43] But in the same interview he affirmed his commitment to the exploration of the problematic limits of the mind, defining the criteria by which he worked as "the degree and quality of consciousness that can be brought to bear on fully liberated materials of the unconscious."[44] In defining his concept of the role of innovative fiction, Hawkes coordinated two imperatives, one relating to the literary tradition, the other to the extra-literary world: "the function of the true innovator or specifically experimental writer is to keep prose alive and constantly to test in the sharpest way possible the range of our human sympathies. . . ."[45]

This coordination was not fortuitous, for the point was that these imperatives are interdependent. The forms of language, as the medium of literary reference to reality, were to be scrutinized for their omissions and distortions. For William Burroughs too, it was a suspicion of language that prompted him to exploit mechanical interventions like the "cut-up method," hoping to subvert the unconscious imposition of received linguistic forms upon the forms of our thinking: "You cannot will spontaneity. But you can introduce the unpredictable spontaneous factor with a pair of scissors."[46] He expressed the hope that such techniques could "show the writer what words are and put him in tactile communication with his medium," not for its own sake, but because only the writer's consciousness of, and experimentation with, the forms of language and of fiction can circumvent the imposition of these forms upon reality itself.[47]

Susan Sontag, who herself wrote two innovative novels (*The Benefactor* and *Death Kit*) in the sixties, similarly advocated the rejuvenation of our sensibility to the forms in which literature presents itself: the neglect of form was an inattention that critical discourse should urgently correct, as she argued in "Against Interpretation." But this was not intended simply to invert the priority of content over form and refuse engagement: "Every writer," she insisted, "works with the idea that this is how it *really* is."[48] Her observations "On Style" illuminated the premise underlying the polemics of "Against Interpretation," that formal decisions are inherently *meaningful*: "every style embodies an epistemological decision, an interpretation of how and what we perceive. . . . Every style is a means of insisting upon something."[49]

If we reconsider the supposed symptoms of the "autonomy" of innovative fiction in the context of specific texts, it is often possible to rediscover their means of engagement in these "symptoms" themselves. In the case of *play*, for example, we might easily cite the very playful seriousness of Thomas Pynchon. *Gravity's Rainbow* has by now received sufficient critical attention to put beyond dispute the meaningful import of that novel's ludic exuberance. But his earlier and slimmer *The Crying of Lot 49* directs its games towards similarly serious ends, and in the process suggests something of the logic of innovative fiction.

The playfulness of *Lot 49* chiefly consists in its multiplication of
"clues" to the mysterious Tristero, its continuous intensification of
both Oedipa's attempts to understand it and the text's orientation
towards narrative resolution; an intensification simultaneously frustrated by the tendency of these clues towards two alternative and
ultimately irreconcilable interpretations. These alternatives, associated
respectively with imagery of apocalyptic revelation and the prison of
solipsism, remain in equilibrium right up to the novel's last sentences,
in a teasing refusal of resolution that leaves Oedipa suspended in
anticipation of the crying of lot 49. The Tristero is that in which
Oedipa intuits the possibility of realities beyond her own narrowly
defined existence, the "exitlessness" of which is imaged in a Reme-
dios Varo painting depicting prisoners in a tower weaving the tapestry
of their entire world. It raises the question of difference, of otherness,
and of the tension between the solipsism of the inviolate individual
and the threat posed to individual identity by community; and it
holds out the paradoxical promise of a community of the alienated
and the dispossessed. Those who have refused, or been refused by,
the standards of conformity enshrined in society's structures of be-
longing—state, corporation, family, every cultural and ideological
norm—appear everywhere to be uniting under the Tristero. Oedipa,
pursuing this promise, exposes herself to the twin threats it implies:
that she will lose herself in the logic of a connectedness become
universal, transcendent and apocalyptic; or that it will resolve into a
product of her own paranoia, confirming her imprisonment in solipsism. What she seeks is a model of connection without assimilation,
of the interaction of discrete systems, by which her needs for connectedness *and* identity can be accommodated. Pynchon presents
several models for such a relationship—the deaf-mute dance, the
Nefastis Machine, the Inamorati Anonymous, Mike Fallopian's community of paranoids. But all are characterized by illogicality or
chance, as the necessary recourse for a mode of connection that is not
paranoid fantasy, nor yet guaranteed by a theological determinism
of cause and effect—the automated predestination Oedipa herself
envisions at the deaf-mute dance. But Oedipa needs positive confirmation, the certainty that is denied her by the very terms of the
double bind in which she must remain to the end of the novel.

Another aspect of Oedipa's dilemma informs the structure of the novel: the question of fiction's relation to reality, which is both invoked and problematized by Pynchon's use of factual information about (for example) Maxwell's Demon and Thurn and Taxis, the obscurity and improbability of which induces uncertainty about the distinction. Fiction, it seems, must be either autonomous or else ubiquitous, at least in terms of representation. But the novel intimates that another model of fictional relation may serve both Oedipa's ends and its own: metaphor. Metaphor offers the possibility of a link between isolated fields that connects but does not conflate. It is metaphor, after all, that underlies the Nefastis Machine, connecting the world of thermodynamics to the world of information flow. But metaphor is not the causal connection Nefastis wants it to be; for the possibility must always remain that it is *only* a metaphor, and there is no absolute transcendent perspective from which to ascertain its truth status: "The act of metaphor then was a thrust at truth and a lie, depending on where you were: inside, safe, or outside, lost. Oedipa did not know where she was."[50] There is an irreducible play in metaphor that Oedipa cannot countenance but Pynchon can; and in his own play casts his lot with metaphor, not representation, as the medium of fiction's "thrust at truth."

The interpretation of *self-consciousness* as an indicator of fictional autonomy would implicate a large proportion of recent American innovative fiction. Self-consciousness of various kinds and degrees is certainly its most prevalent feature—largely because it is virtually inherent in the decision to circumvent the still normative conventions of realism. It may (but need not) imply playfulness, immanence and self-reference (metafiction), so it is difficult to exemplify adequately; but certainly one of the most resolutely self-conscious of recent American novelists is Raymond Federman. In his fiction, this question of self-consciousness was always inscribed as a response to a very particular reality, in relation to which it stood as a perpetual digression, as the enacted evasion of a central event marked only as "(X-X-X-X)": the extermination of his family at Auschwitz. But this specific application of the evasiveness for which self-conscious fiction is generally condemned in fact serves to empower it, so that as Charles Caramello has argued, "the central event in Federman's fiction is not the extermination of his family but the erasure of that extermination as a central event."[51] By redoubling the strategy, making his self-consciousness itself the argument of his narrative as he does in *The Voice in the Closet* (1979), Federman is able to pursue and articulate its fictional logic and the reality it seeks to contain (include *and* control) with an extraordinary intensity. In contrast to the visual exuberance of *Double or Nothing* (1971) and *Take It or Leave It* (1976), he makes the text of *The Voice in the Closet* a typographic equivalent of the closet in which he was hidden as a boy to escape the Nazis, and also of the text's own imprisonment within the paradox of its confrontation and evasion of this escape: the English text consists of twenty full pages of eighteen perfectly justified unpunctuated lines; the French text, of twenty-two of fourteen. The narrative tells the story of the boy entombed in the closet and of the man he becomes, who has closeted himself in a room in the attempt to articulate that story. The narrative "I" is the boy, whose "he" refers to the man by whom his story is written. Within this paradoxical framework the text draws out a series of antithetical equivalences between the two: the boy's escape is inextricable from the loss of his family, just as the man's necessary evasion involves his loss of that loss itself; the boy's guilt at his escape equates with the man's guilt at his dissociation from that guilt; the boy is pushed into the closet to escape history, while the man confines himself in order to confront the history of that escape. The situation emerges as a closed circle of escape and imprisonment, each of which implies the other, and both of which are signified by the closet that contains both narrative and narrator.

Federman's next novel, *The Twofold Vibration* (1982), is by contrast formally loose, being the story of "the old man" narrated by "Federman" from the reports of "Moinous" and "Namredef." The dissolution of the self which was begun in the intense, self-cancelling structure of the previous work is here casually achieved, all four characters possessing some degree of authorial identity. *The Voice in the Closet* itself is inscribed within this novel, attributed to the old man, and this framing procedure is indicative of the way *The Twofold Vibration* relocates the circularity of its predecessor outside the self. By reconstructing the temporality of this cyclic reflexiveness Federman slyly proposes to historicize it: "Hey you guys wake up, wake up, it's starting all over again, but this time it's going to be serious, the real story, no more evasions, procrastinations, and you won't believe this, it begins in the future. . . ."[52] In the future in question, the old man is about to be deported to the space colonies, the novel being an urgent enquiry into his past in order to establish why. By constructing a fictional analogue of the Holocaust, from which and to which the old man's life inexorably leads, Federman is able to map the circularity of his fiction onto history: the novel's title (taken from Beckett) codifies its method, signifying the continuous emergence of the future out of the present's orientation towards the past. The text remains self-cancelling, but its vibrations resonate outwards, since its circularity as narrative does not imply a circular argument. The old man, having been inexplicably condemned to deportation, is as inexplicably finally passed over: his life-story is patterned upon repetition rather than resolution, but its narration articulates, beyond the stasis of this cycle, the old man's progress through history.

If the distinguishing feature of *immanence* in fiction is taken to be the independence of the sign from the (now irrelevant) logic of its representations, then Richard Brautigan's *Trout Fishing in America* would be an excellent example. Brautigan's language often functions as a misdirection of his subject material rather than as its articulation: his similes provoke as much thought about the nature of simile as about their purported reference by straining against the limits of the logic of relation by which the trope operates: "the trout would wait there like airplane tickets."[53] The extremity of the cultural distance between vehicle and tenor supplants the ground upon which they are united (even if one is to be found) as the focus of attention. Brautigan's metaphors similarly subvert rather than enhance the narrative, often persisting beyond the occasion of their use to become literalized elements of the narrative situation. Brautigan's figurative language doesn't follow the narrative world it describes in *Trout Fishing in America,* but leads it. The result is not an accent upon language in its pristine self-sufficiency, but rather upon the culture it encodes, and by which it is circumscribed. There emerges a narrative sensibility that represents the relation between the narrator and America as itself paradigmatic of this condition. The novel is characterized by a sense of loss, a wry nostalgia for an unspoilt America: the humour often communicates an underlying bitterness which is not addressed simply towards the contaminated, technological, commercialized America it describes but also towards the image of nature it evokes in counterpoint. The ideal of trout fishing that provides the centre for the book's nostalgia represents a harmony with nature which it knows to be an impossible dream, and denies in its writing: its language in itself constitutes the distance articulated in the extremity of the novel's attempts to overcome it. Language is the condition of culture at the price of nature: the question becomes one of the value of the culture inscribed in the language. Brautigan's evaluation is bleak, discovering atrophied sensibilities at every turn. "Expressing a human need," he proposes to end the book with the word "mayonnaise." The "Mayonnaise Chapter" that follows consists of a letter of condolence entirely made up of the formulaic, empty language of bereavement: an irrelevant postscript misspells the crucial word. The design is frustrated by a failure of language, which is also the failure of culture upon which the design was predicated.

All this is not to say that innovative writers remained innocent of the critical expectations brought to their work: some of them, after all, were partly responsible for creating these expectations. The point is not that innovative fiction is *as such* valuably and significantly engaged, but that (again, as such) it can be, and manifestly has been. A climate of uncritical acceptance inevitably produced some innovative fictions that were insubstantial or frivolous. But the critical backlash also provoked an increasingly self-critical attitude among innovative novelists, who expressed, in their work and in their public statements, a greater emphasis upon the capacity of innovative fiction to offer formally sophisticated means of confronting substantial social, political and cultural themes. This shift of emphasis should be understood as a validation of their methods, not an implicit admission of guilt: it was simply an affirmation of innovative fiction's ability to achieve fresh and diverse literary contemplations of the real world—the end for which the cause of innovation had generally been adopted from the beginning.

The paradigm for this shift in the attitude of innovative writers is provided by Donald Barthelme's two essays, "After Joyce" and "Not-

Knowing." In the earlier (1964) essay, Barthelme articulated the idea of the literary work as an object in its own right, not merely the medium of the author's vision of reality: "The reader is not listening to an authoritative account of the world delivered by an expert (Faulkner on Mississippi, Hemingway on the corrida) but bumping into something that is *there*, like a rock or a refrigerator."[54] In "Not-Knowing," Barthelme disowned this opinion, in order to place a greater emphasis on the writer's confrontation of reality: "I suggest that art is always a meditation upon external reality rather than a representation of external reality or a jackleg attempt to 'be' external reality. . . . Twenty years ago I was much more convinced of the autonomy of the literary object than I am now, and even wrote a rather persuasive defense of the proposition that I have just rejected: that the object is itself world."[55] In fact, "After Joyce" was not a flat declaration of the autonomy of the literary object, but an assertion of its actuality. The essay did assert art's capacity for engagement with reality: "The artist's effort, always and everywhere, is to attain a fresh mode of cognition. . . . Far from implying a literature that is its own subject matter, the work that is an object is rich in possibilities. The intention of the artist may range in any direction, including those directions which have the approval of socially-minded critics. What is important is that he has placed himself in a position to gain access to a range of meanings previously inaccessible to his art."[56] The shift was a response to the changing critical environment, and was less a question of substance than of emphasis. In the later essay Barthelme gave rather more attention to arguing the engagement of his concept of art, as neither a representation of reality nor an alternative to it: "Art is a true account of the activity of mind. Because consciousness, in Husserl's formulation, is always consciousness *of* something, art thinks ever of the world, cannot not think of the world, could not turn its back on the world even if it wished to."[57] Nor is this a glib formula designed to release the writer from any further responsibility, but a firm declaration of duty: "The aim of meditating about the world is finally to change the world. It is this meliorative aspect of literature that provides its ethical dimension."[58]

CRITICISM ABOUT CRITICISM

In the same essay, at the same time as the *Mississippi Review* was
hailing the new minimalism, Barthelme was himself toying with the
prospect of the "New Thing": "So we have a difficulty. What shall
we call the New Thing, which I haven't encountered yet but which
is bound to be out there somewhere? Post-Postmodernism sounds, to
me, a little lumpy. . . . It should have the word *new* in it somewhere.
The New Newness? Or maybe the Post-New?"[59] Barthelme's benign
satire mocked the general critical preoccupation with literary succession, but its real target was the concept of postmodernism itself. It
was under the rubric of postmodernism, above all else, that innovative fiction had been homogenized and stigmatized through the seventies and eighties; yet it was the critical concept, not the fiction, that
created the problem. As Barthelme's parodic musings suggest, it is a
concept riddled with paradox, even in name. If its various formulations and formulators can be said to have anything in common it is
some sort of reaction against the order enshrined in the antecedent
concept of modernism. This is an entirely negative position—the
denial of that order—nor can it have a positive content without
violating its own premises by establishing itself as a rival order, in the
image of its enemy. But the conceptual opposition *itself* tends to
establish postmodernism, insofar as it is advanced as a concept, on the
same footing as modernism, and so implicates it in a fundamental
paradox. As a *concept,* it can only be an exercise in self-negation; yet
if it is once allowed a descriptive validity, this self-negation becomes
an attribute foisted upon its designated cultural manifestations. This, I
would suggest, is the critical violence that the concept of postmodernism has done to innovative fiction: it has subordinated that fiction
to the logic of a grand cultural hypothesis; and then, finding the
hypothesis embroiled in self-contradiction, it has delegated responsibility for its paralysis back to the fiction itself.

I do not wish to deny the validity of any theoretical debate on the
question of modernism and postmodernism, which is far more complex than this caricature implies. Its permutations have been explored
by Fredric Jameson, who has elaborated four possible theoretical

alignments: two (antimodernist/propostmodernist and promodernist/
antipostmodernist) assert the dichotomy of their terms; the other two
(pro(post)modernist and anti(post)modernist) emphasize their continuity. Each of these positions is furthermore capable of sustaining
both politically progressive and reactionary orientations, and Jameson
even found these could coexist in the same theory.[60] Clearly, such an
opposition can sustain considerable debate at a high level of abstraction, a debate which has its own kind of validity and rigour. But
given the primacy—the autonomy—of the theoretical domain in this
debate, that rigour has not extended to its use of the phenomena
upon which it purports to be founded, and to which it should be
answerable. This is most flagrantly the case with "postmodern(ist)
fiction," the critical currency of which has released it from any
obligation to represent its supposed manifestations, and allowed it
instead to measure *their* adequacy to its own formula. In the shift from
a diagnostic to a categoric function the concept has been released
from its interpretative foundations, and particular works become clas-
sifiable as more or less "postmodern."

This problem is general, and arises whenever conceptual abstractions become themselves the centre of critical debate. A good example of its consequences in the criticism of fiction was the postmodernism of Brian McHale, which betrayed the inadequacy of the concept
precisely because it did attempt to retain the link between its meta-
physical conceptual framework and a large number of illustrative
fictions—although the interest was still centred upon the construct,
postmodernism, rather than upon the phenomena to which it referred.[61] McHale accumulated a repertoire of techniques and ploys
that supported his definition of postmodernism, which involved the
foregrounding of ontological questions as a self-reflexive step beyond
the more epistemological scepticism of modernism; but the particular
uses that were made of these techniques were lost in the generality of
an ultraformalism. Only in his last chapter did he address the question
of the potential for "aboutness" of postmodernism, in response to
Gerald Graff. He argued that it was about love and death; yet his
argument remained wholly bound within the generality of form. So,
he claimed that postmodernist writing "models or simulates death; it
produces simulacra of death through confrontations between worlds,

through transgressions of ontological levels or boundaries, or through vacillation between different kinds and degrees of 'reality.' "[62] This "aboutness" derived wholly from formal strategies, and was achieved without descending to the specifics of the text (or indeed the specifics of the themes he invoked). McHale's postmodern techniques were conceived of autonomously, not as the means by which a specific text might conduct its argument. As a result his attention to specific texts turned into a device-ridden catalogue of formalist clichés.

Other critics who elaborated concepts of postmodernism with particular reference to fiction found alternative ways to formulate the distinction from modernism. Alan Wilde, for example, traced through modernism and postmodernism the rearguard action of irony as a mode of human accommodation to chaos. The shift from modernism to postmodernism was conceived of as a shift of emphasis: modernist irony was the means of establishing a unitary aesthetic order in the face of a fallen world, while postmodernist "suspensive irony" relinquishes this desire for control, and "abandons the quest for paradise altogether—the world in all its disorder is simply (or not so simply) accepted."[63] He perceived in this acceptance the basis from which a "generative reaction" could be developed, establishing contingent meanings and values through provisional frameworks of order as the basis for a quietly affirmative "assent." To this extent Wilde set limits to the logic of his own argument: his principle of irony drew upon a broadly phenomenological theoretical background that predicated a relatively unproblematic subject as the embattled ironist. But for Charles Russell the self, considered as the last secure totality in the modern subjective aesthetic, broke down under postmodern scrutiny. He offered the general diagnosis that "If there is a dominant focus to postmodern American fiction, it is the problematical nature of the subjective presence . . . whether subjectivity is seen in terms of character, writer, or the voice of the text as language. . . ."[64] He contrasted postmodernism with modernism in terms of four oppositions, formulated as individual and culture, personal speech and collective discourse, specific text and literary convention, and literature and society's semiotic codes: "Whereas the practises of modernism and the early avant-garde emphasised the relative independence and privileged perspective of the first term of each of these

sets . . . postmodern thought recognises the effective primacy of the
latter terms out of which, against which, but always within which
individual subjects, voices, texts, or codes must articulate themselves."[65] As it was brought within the influence of those terms over
which it had held a transcendent position in the modernist perspective (and in Wilde), the self was brought into question; and this
implication of the "self," everywhere and at all levels, is that which
denies the concept of postmodernism itself any identity.

Because all these critical arguments were conducted within a general, abstract frame, they dealt less with fictions than with their
attributes: the fictions themselves were thereby rendered mute, and
only the critical discourse remained articulate. This in itself confined
the fiction concerned to the "symptom" side of criticism's symptom/
critique dichotomy: there was no possibility of distinguishing, in
terms of these postmodern attributes, between fictions that problematized them and those that simply manifested them. As purely conceptual counters, the attributes concerned belonged to the discourse of
criticism. From which it followed that, unless they were disavowed
and presented in the context of a critique, the criticism itself necessarily became a symptomatic discourse. So that just as all these versions
of postmodernism turned upon the erosion of equivalent modernist
certainties, they eroded the positions from which they were themselves articulated. It is not surprising that the dominant characteristic
of the various concepts of postmodernism has been the way they
themselves undermine and critique their status as concepts.

This feature of theories of postmodernism was epitomized in that
of Jean-François Lyotard, who took its defining trait to be a crisis of
legitimation—a loss of belief in the authority upon which a society's
ruling narratives are based. In *The Postmodern Condition* he analysed
this crisis and sought to articulate the forms of legitimation compatible with postmodern scepticism. Lyotard understood the postmodern
to be "the state of our culture following the transformations which,
since the end of the nineteenth century, have altered the game rules
for science, literature and the arts," implying a relationship with
modernism other than the common one of temporal succession.[66] In
fact the terms in which he contrasted the two in "Answering the
Question: What Is Postmodernism?" implied that postmodernism

was for him a species of avant-gardism, always on the run from the ossification of a modernism that followed rather than preceded it. In terms of the "incredulity toward metanarratives" by which he succinctly characterised his postmodernism, he conceived of the postmodern as sharing with the modern this sceptical nature ("It is undoubtedly part of the modern. All that has been received, if only yesterday . . . must be suspected"), but made a paradoxical distinction: "A work can become modern only if it is first postmodern. Postmodernism thus understood is not modernism at its end but in the nascent state, and this state is constant."[67] The logical sequence is the reverse of the chronological sequence. Modernism begins by sharing postmodernism's incredulity, but transgresses from the "nascent state," the leading edge constantly maintained in postmodernism, to the consolation of a stable aesthetic form. Postmodernism, by contrast, is vigilant in its suspicion even of its own form: "Modern aesthetics . . . allows the unpresentable to be put forward only as the missing contents; but the form, because of its recognizable consistency, continues to offer the reader or viewer matter for solace and pleasure. The postmodern would be that which, in the modern, puts forward the unpresentable in presentation itself; that which denies itself the solace of good forms, the consensus of a taste which would make it possible to share the nostalgia for the unattainable."[68]

Any attempt to determine where this argument leaves Lyotard's own discourse encounters an impasse: it is itself a metanarrative that—precisely to the extent that it is legitimate—delegitimizes itself. Lyotard's uneasiness about this paradox was evident at the end of his dialogue with Jean-Loup Thébaud, *Just Gaming*. Here Lyotard argued for a concept of legitimation within the multiplicity of language games, each with their own specific rules; but then he appealed to a *universal* framework of justice in order to guarantee this multiplicity. Thébaud's response "Here you are talking like the great prescriber himself . . . (laughter)," concluded the book, and the theory's paradoxical status is implicit in their laughter: Lyotard had no other reply.[69] This theoretical paralysis does not simply refute the concept of postmodernism, but it renders it strangely intransitive; and this intransitiveness affects not only postmodern theoretical discourse's capacity for engagement, but also the capacity of dissenting discourses to engage with it.

The theorist who has attempted most resolutely to engage the concept of postmodernism from without is Fredric Jameson. He sought to preserve the exteriority of his own discourse by framing the attributes of postmodernism as symptoms of the "cultural logic of late capitalism." In particular, he invoked such cultural manifestations as "schizophrenia," understood (after Lacan) as a language disorder in which there occurs a breakdown of the relationship between signifiers; and "pastiche," meaning a parodic form that lacks the implication of a norm against which its deviance can be measured (characteristic of the immanence of media, after Baudrillard). The rootlessness of these conditions, he suggested, encourages a cultural eclecticism that functions effectively as an effacement of history, a politically paralysing "fragmentation of time into a series of perpetual presents."[70] Accordingly, Jameson confronted the concept of postmodernism in order "to see whether by systematizing something that is resolutely unsystematic, and historicizing something that is resolutely ahistorical, one couldn't outflank it and force a historical way at least of thinking about that."[71] His "at least" is telling: Jameson did not seek to contest the ahistorical version of contemporary cultural phenomena enshrined in postmodernist theory, but only to contest, upon that premise, the ahistoricity of the theory itself. This attempt to "outflank" postmodernism put Jameson outside the frame of its descriptive enterprise yet simultaneously (since he recognized that "postmodernism theory . . . is clearly a class which is a member of its own class"[72]) trapped him within the paradoxes of that enterprise. His argument was ensnared within the concept of postmodernism even in opposition to it: however self-contradictory the term was, he argued, "we cannot *not* use it. But . . . every time it is used, we are under the obligation to rehearse those inner contradictions and to stage those representational inconsistencies and dilemmas."[73]

To recast this argument in a context more specific to innovative American fiction, one might consider the arguments of Gerald Graff and Ihab Hassan. In Graff's terms, the concept of postmodernism was to be seen as the final stage in a degeneration of the foundations of meaning that could be traced all the way through romanticism and modernism. This he mapped out as a long retreat into subjectivism, aestheticism and ultimately self-cancelling fabulous nihilism, which left the postmodern novelist incapable of claiming any critical engagement with social reality. The distortion involved in Graff's perspective was apparent when he came to consider individual writers, and had to concede that such indispensable figures to any postmodern canon as John Barth and Donald Barthelme need not be understood symptomatically, "in sociological terms," but were "actually concerned with society."[74] But the fact of this engagement, and the question of whether it need be understood in terms of the objective standards Graff wanted to reassert, was dismissed in the course of his argument with the *concept*. It did serve to demonstrate the concept's failure to engage with its referents: but because he took the concept for the literature it was incapable, in its paradoxical self-sufficiency, of adequately representing, he simultaneously represented this very failure as a failure of the literature's *own* engagement with reality.

Ihab Hassan's more enthusiastic embrace of the concept of postmodernism combined the impulse towards abstraction that the term generally stimulated with an abnormal zeal for categorization. His work has been dominated by taxonomical schemes for the subdivision of his master-concept, which functioned less to demonstrate its coherence than to exhaust its multiplicity. Nor did he hesitate to acknowledge this multiplicity, because this in itself was incorporated into his definition of postmodernism: the heterogeneity of its referents became, in fact, a measure of their homogeneity. These taxonomical schemes replaced any engagement with actual cultural phenomena, and provided a simulacrum of reciprocity between the abstract and the concrete that released his concept from any problematic criterion of truth. It was his lists, rather than the literature they designated, that formed the intuitive base from which abstract speculations were launched—and to which they returned, as if for confirmation. This circularity, which framed the whole of Hassan's enterprise, rendered his concept of postmodernism inaccessible to the sceptic, even as it was self-evident to the believer. The unifying concept, always to be defined, was already defining the terms within which, in an increasingly hermetic series of books, Hassan explored and elaborated it.

In shoring up his concept of postmodernism, Hassan repeatedly enacted a form of preemptive self-criticism, but one that in the process was incorporated into the concept itself, and accordingly served only to reinforce it. So, he offered a list of "Ten conceptual problems that both conceal and constitute postmodernism itself."[75] "Conceal" *and* "constitute" because although formulated as problems, these ten points functioned in themselves to give notional definition to the concept they undermined. This effect, reduced to its most concise form, had the character of rhetorical sleight-of-hand: by purporting to address the conceptual problems associated with post-modernism, he had already established its existence. Similarly, Hassan's schematic table of differences between modernism and post-modernism embraced oppositions so diverse and allusive as to defy summary, but certainly deserving Susan Suleiman's complaint that they break down badly when applied to "actual texts."[76] Hassan had anticipated her objection, however, and qualified his schematization: "concepts in any one vertical column are not all equivalent; and inversions and exceptions, in both modernism and postmodernism, abound. Still, I would submit that rubrics in the right column point to the postmodern tendency."[77] More direct would have been to say they *are* the postmodern tendency: the concept, thus defined, had become a priori, and specific texts were simply more or less adequate manifestations of it. And since the concept had itself incorporated enough exemplary self-contradictions to furnish its own paradoxical logic, Hassan's postmodernism had effectively outgrown its referents and become autonomous.

Linda Hutcheon was one critic who sought to reconcile the para-doxical nature of postmodernism with a sense of social and historical engagement: The required balance between reference and self-reflexiveness, she suggested, could be maintained by *parody,* which "is a perfect postmodernist form in some senses, for it paradoxically both incorporates and challenges that which it parodies."[78] Parody could be extended to allow the appropriation not just of superseded narrative modes, but also of the framework of stable meaning and values that enabled straightforward engagement with reality. To maintain its insights into the rhetorical nature of truth without simply conceding the domain of truth to those who believed otherwise, it was necessary that "The contradictions of both postmodernist theory and practice are positioned within the system and yet work to allow its premises to be seen as fictions or as ideological structures. This does not necessarily destroy their 'truth' value, but it does define the conditions of that 'truth.' "[79] But by the same token this logic of a "contradictory relationship of constant slippage" defied any attempt to locate an essential concept, "postmodernism," as Hutcheon was compelled to acknowledge: "In writing about these postmodernist contradictions, then, I clearly would not want to fall into the trap of suggesting any 'transcendental identity' or essence for postmodernism. I see it as an ongoing cultural process or activity. . . ."[80] No concept, then, only process or activity. In focusing upon the paradoxical qualities by which she defined postmodernism, Hutcheon in effect performed the necessary critical short-circuit. Her argument involved a refusal of the concept of postmodernism as such, and hence the invalidation of any debate in which that concept is a predicate.

This emphasis upon process returns us to Lyotard's description of postmodernism as prior rather than posterior to modernism, where the emphasis was upon the continuity of this condition through time: it "is not modernism at its end but in the nascent state, *and this state is constant*."[81] This postmodernism is effectively an avant-gardism accelerated to a condition of flux. It implies a proliferation of revisionary perspectives beyond the parameters of a monolinear cultural heritage in which the old order is inexorably superseded by a new orthodoxy. But in these terms, any attempt to affirm the *totality* of these cultural discourses would be precisely such a new orthodoxy, and therefore at once self-contradictory. And *as* a totality, such a discourse must be regarded as merely symptomatic of prevailing cultural conditions: this was exactly the charge Lyotard levelled at Charles Jencks's postmodern "transavantgardism" in architecture, the eclecticism of which he considered merely a reflection of capital's power to accommodate indiscriminately all tendencies to its purpose.[82] But clearly, Lyotard's own overarching concept of postmodernism must self-destruct, or else be exposed to the same objection.

FICTION ABOUT FICTION?

The diversity of innovative fiction was obliterated in a pincer movement executed by criticism's forces of unification: on the one hand it suffered the a priori, rationalist imposition of the blanket theoretical label "postmodernism"; on the other it was subjected to the aggrandizement of the empirical category of metafiction. The inevitable result of this process was the meeting and synonymy of metafiction and postmodernism: Linda Hutcheon even declared that "the term 'postmodernism' seems to me to be a very limiting label for such a broad contemporary phenomenon as metafiction."[83] Such homogenization has been the blight of innovative fiction's critical reputation, reducing a whole spectrum of arguments to a repetitive set of variations upon a single theme. In fact, I would argue that the number of innovative fictions that can justly be labelled "metafictions" is actually very small; but I would also argue that metafiction, properly understood, has nothing to do with autonomy. I have just claimed that the self-referentiality of the critical discourse of postmodernism disengaged it from the fiction it purported to represent, so I would appear bound to accept a similar argument regarding metafictional self-referentiality. But there is actually an important sense in which "fiction about fiction" works in the opposite direction to the "criticism about criticism" that overwhelms postmodernist critical discourse: for while that discourse continues to claim a grasp upon actual cultural conditions even as it spirals into self-referential paradox, metafiction *begins* in self-reference in order to generate the terms of its engagement. This engagement is in fact enabled by the fundamentally different means available to it *as fiction*.

It is of course possible that a text may take fiction not only as its frame of reference, but also as the actual question it seeks to engage: this should be acknowledged at the outset. William Gass's *Willie Masters' Lonesome Wife*, in Larry McCaffery's description, "a remarkably pure and interesting example of the genre," must be understood in such terms, so that to take it as representative is to concede almost everything in advance to the autonomous view of metafiction.[84] The book appears to assert its autonomy at every turn: in its material presence as object (it is divided into four sections printed on blue, olive, red and glossy white paper respectively); in the host of typographical devices it indulges; and in its insistence upon the texture of language as pure sound.[85] This is not to say that the book lacks a "literal" narrative: with a degree of heavy-handedness it is possible to interpret the book as an exploration of the frustrated sexuality of a

midwestern housewife, Babs, through the story of her unsatisfactory
relationship with her lover Phil Gelvin. But to do so would be to
misunderstand its import, and in fact to invert the literal-metaphorical
hierarchy of the narrative. It is the nature of fiction, not the story of
Babs, that is the focus of the book, and Babs's status in relation to
this is exactly that of a metaphor in a realistic novel—its function
subordinate, and its realization ephemeral. The relationship between
Babs and Gelvin is a metaphor for both the relation of writer to work
and that of text to reader. Language, the medium Gass makes so
tangible, is the common ground between the two analogies: as the
intractable material of the writer, it is the insensitive lover; as the
literary text frustrated by an unresponsive reader, it is the sensuous
unfulfilled woman.

   Does this constitute fictional autonomy? At the end of the text, a
ring representing the stain of a coffee cup encircles the words "YOU
HAVE FALLEN INTO ART—RETURN TO LIFE." It is as clear a
statement of the separation of fiction and reality as could be wished
for, but even so it succinctly refutes the autonomy of the fiction that
contains it. "Art" in this sentence is a referent, placing the sentence
itself in a critical relation to art. That is the nature of metafiction: the
turning of fictional attention upon itself generates a meta-level of
attention. Of course this level can be incorporated by becoming itself
the object of attention, but this generates a further level, meaning
that there is always a level of attention which is conceptually posterior
to the act of fiction, and in that sense outside it. Metafiction, then, is
never absolutely self-referential, for the metafictional work in its
entirety must always be larger than the fictional element of itself to
which it has a meta-relation. Even in *Willie Masters' Lonesome Wife*
there remains a distinction between means and ends: it is not these
categories which have been collapsed into a monistic self-sufficiency,
but the genres of fiction and criticism. The book is essentially an
extension of the enterprise Gass had undertaken in his critical essays,
that of affirming the medium of language in literature; its peculiar
characteristic is that it functions as its own exemplum. Nor is the
aesthetic argument embodied in *Willie Masters' Lonesome Wife* itself
anti-referential, but affirms on its last page that the aesthetic pleasure
of language is, after all, an *expressive* pleasure.

In fact, *Willie Masters' Lonesome Wife* is almost unique in using self-referential techniques in the service of an argument that is indeed ultimately concerned with fiction: it can do no more than hint at the capacity for engagement of metafictions that direct their self-referentiality towards other ends. But even here the idea that metafiction is inherently autonomous—a brush that tarred every innovative fiction to which the term was (legitimately and illegitimately) applied—proves inapplicable. Nonetheless, from the late sixties onwards fictions that included overtly self-referential passages, like *Snow White* (1967), *Pricksongs and Descants* (1969), *The Exagggerations of Peter Prince* (1968), *Double or Nothing* (1971), *Lost in the Funhouse* (1968), and, most pertinently titled, *The Death of the Novel and Other Stories* (1969), were widely understood to have *replaced* fiction's attention to reality with fiction's attention to itself, rather than superimposing the latter *upon* the former. Self-referentiality became synonymous with autonomy.

There is a reciprocity between the tendency to regard almost any nonrealistic novel as metafiction and the tendency to treat metafictions as autonomous: the looseness of definition that allows the genre to expand indiscriminately also obscures the specific means of engagement it employs. It is important to distinguish between a novel that employs occasional metafictional devices and one to which metafiction is essential, and which can therefore be designated *a* metafiction; between truly metafictional self-*reference,* in which the medium is incorporated as subject, and more general self-*consciousness,* in which it is simply acknowledged; and between fictions that are avowedly metafictional and those that are only rendered so by the violence of critical interpretation. Typologists of metafiction seeking to define its range and limits often blurred such distinctions, unwilling to confine the genre so closely that its significance was diminished. Linda Hutcheon, for example, identified four categories of "narrative narcissism," respectively characterized by overt or covert linguistic or diegetic self-reflection. The covert linguistic category implied such devices as anagrams, cryptograms and lipograms which, insofar as they can be said not to call attention to themselves, are less the marks of a metafictional text than evidence of a metafictional consciousness in the act of composition—and what act of composition ever lacked

such a consciousness? The covert diegetic category was characterized
by forms—the detective story, fantasy, game structure and the
erotic—that were in some way inherently suggestive as parallels for
the form of narrative: but the point at which these parallels, without
being overtly drawn, became significant enough to render the text
metafictional remained obscure. This concept of metafiction was
greatly expanded by Sarah Lauzen, to the extent that she could cite
William Gaddis's *JR* (1975) as a metafiction, on the grounds that
it exhibited "reduced narration" and "reduced structure."[86] These
qualities were deemed metafictional because they highlight narrative
conventions not by commenting upon them but by neglecting them.
Clearly the more reasonable interpretation would be that *JR* is antithetical to metafiction—that its art is not innovative in a self-reflexive
way but in the extremity to which it takes the logic of mimesis. *JR* is
almost entirely dialogue, written as if it were really transcribed speech,
with all its incoherence, redundancy, hesitation and fragmentation.
The effect of such extreme fidelity to the forms of speech is to
dehumanize it, presenting it as a stream of language which communicates in inverse ratio to its length. It offers progressively less information and more noise; the interference of the several discourses that
meet in the novel—legal, social, technological, economic, political—
results in degraded communication between the characters and a
consequent loss of human agency. This is the burden of the novel's
central plot line, the more or less automatic growth and collapse of
the eleven-year-old JR's business empire. Without understanding
much more than the profit motive that drives both his school and his
society, JR triggers the mechanisms of the stock market and free
enterprise and is then carried along by the process. Thomas LeClair
has described the novel in terms of a "runaway system," in which
process supersedes agency, and shows how this structure to the plot
of the book is enacted in its form.[87] It might be further argued that
the same structure also obtains in the way the novel relates to reality,
in its pursuit of representation to excess—the principle of mimesis
itself becomes a runaway system and so an obstacle to representation.
JR both defamiliarizes the reality of contemporary America and mimics the processes that, it is the novel's argument, constitute that reality.
This then is a fictional strategy absolutely opposite to metafiction:

fiction that presents itself as an equivalent system to reality—not a fiction about fiction but a reality about reality.

Lauzen did go some way towards delimiting the field in one respect, by formulating her definition of metafiction so as to exclude texts in which self-reference is an incidental phenomenon: "Metafiction uses techniques to *systematically* heighten its own status as fiction."[88] This defined the formal qualities that constitute metafiction, but stopped short of articulating their functional orientation: texts that heighten their own status as fiction are not fictions *about* fiction, but only fictions that declare themselves to be such. An adequate definition requires some further qualification such as that provided by Patricia Waugh: "*Metafiction* is a term given to fiction writing which self-consciously and systematically draws attention to its status as an artefact *in order to pose questions about the relationship between fiction and reality.*"[89] The last clause does two things: it makes it clear that a metafiction has a specifiable orientation both formally *and* thematically; and it contradicts the implication in "fiction about fiction" of a closed, autotelic loop, since the "aboutness" is equally inherent in the final term of this description, which should be read "fiction about fiction about reality."

The taxonomical expansion of metafiction as a category was complemented by the expansion of its thematic scope in Larry McCaffery's *The Metafictional Muse,* which advocated a more generous definition of "fiction." Unlike the approaches of other commentators on metafiction, this strategy was not meant to extend the formal criteria of the genre, but to enlarge its frame of reference. "Fiction" was equated with all nonobjective cognitive structures, those "subjective (i.e., *fictional*) forms developed to organize our relationship to the world in a coherent fashion."[90] To write about such forms was therefore to write metafiction, and the metafictionist was reassimilated to the mainstream of socially engaged literature. As a defence of metafiction, this denial of its thematic specificity made no more sense than the denial of its formal restrictions in Hutcheon's and Lauzen's definitions. And like their approaches, it succeeded only in stigmatizing a much larger range of innovative fictions with the pejorative associations of metafiction. But while Hutcheon and Lauzen implicitly accepted the charges against metafiction in the stricter sense,

McCaffery's argument at least pointed the way to refute them, albeit in the process of eclipsing the genre's distinctive orientation. The designation of all imposed cognitive structures as "fictions" obscured the fact that the evident parallels between fiction and such structures were especially susceptible to examination through the *self-referential* quality possessed by metafiction in its narrow sense, and dissipated by McCaffery's definition. Self-reference involves the frame-breaking process of self-transcendence, and this manoeuvre generates the dislocation of perspective to which metafiction owes its unique analytical insights.

An example might be John Barth's *Lost in the Funhouse,* generally taken to epitomize (for good or ill) the characteristics of metafiction. The shortest story in the book is "Frame-Tale," which defines the fictional space of metafiction as a Möbius strip in which the words "ONCE UPON A TIME THERE WAS A STORY THAT BEGAN" perform an infinite framing process upon themselves.[91] This seems to be a concise image of the endless, inescapable fictionality for which metafiction has repeatedly been condemned. But the formation of a Möbius strip involves a twist: because the strip has no verso, it openly presents itself as one-sided. This story doesn't not end, so much as it never stops beginning: it never completes a frame, and so is less a fiction *from* which we can never escape, than one *into* which we can never escape.

The book's longest story, "Menelaiad," is constructed as seven frames of the narrative of Menelaus, the storyteller-lover: the voice that now constitutes Menelaus narrates Menelaus narrating to Telemachus and Peisistratus Menelaus narrating to Helen at Pharos Menelaus narrating to Proteus Menelaus narrating to Eidothea Menelaus narrating to Helen at Troy the story of their love. " ' " 'Hard tale to hold onto, this' " ' " (143), declares Helen, anticipating Menelaus's attempt to grasp the shape-shifting Proteus, which becomes the paradigm of his (and the tale's) attempt to pin the forms of narrative and experience to some ultimate truth, to maintain the exteriority of the teller or lover to his tale or love. Through that parallel, embodied in Menelaus himself, the story engages the conflict between hierarchies of control in sexual relations, and the unsettling reciprocity implied in an ideal of mutual love. The heart of the narrative is Helen's choice of mediocre Menelaus from among all the princes of Greece, and his question on their wedding night: why? Helen's answer, "Love," breaks the frame within which Menelaus contains his world and his tale: his love for her contains her, making her *his* reality; but her love for him reverses this ontological hierarchy of creator and created: " ' " ' " ' "To love is easy; to be loved, as if one were real, on the order of others: fearsome mystery!" ' " ' " ' " (156). Pursuing the mystery to the oracle at Delphi (on the recommendation of Paris) he confronts the abyss—" ' " ' " ' " '   ' " ' " ' " ' " (158)—and recoils: " ' " ' " ' "Poste-haste he returned to Lacedemon, done with questions. He'd re-embrace his terrifying chooser, clasp her past speech, never let go, frig understanding; it would be bride-night, endless; their tale would rebegin. 'Menelaus here!' His shout shook the wifeless hall" ' " ' " ' " (158). Instead the tale begins to end. He recovers Helen from Troy, and tries to accept (having held him fast through his entire repertoire of transformations) Proteus's laconic advice: " ' " ' "Let go" ' " ' " (161). But a doubt remains: in the final phase of their struggle, Menelaus had found himself clasping nothing, or air—or himself. His encounter with Proteus too precisely mirrors his struggle with the reciprocity of love to offer reassurance. And Helen promptly undermines the authority of his repossession by announcing the unreality of the Helen who went to Troy, a cloud-Helen sent in her place by Hermes. Constrained by his own love to accept the declared faithfulness of hers, Menelaus casts aside all scepticism; but the doubt cannot be excised, and even as his tale is told back in Sparta, he has to face the possibility that Telemachus has crept away in the dark to cuckold him once more. The contingency remains, the impossibility of extricating the teller from his tale, the lover from his love. Yet the paradox of his struggle with Proteus has not evaporated the reality he would contain, but rather the self that would contain it. As the frames close, and this self-reflexive logic works itself out, what ultimately remains is not a solipsism of the self, or of fiction: "Then when as must at last every tale, all tellers, all told, Menelaus's story itself in ten or ten thousand years expires, yet I'll survive it, I, in Proteus's terrifying last disguise, Beauty's spouse's odd Elysium: the absurd, unending possibility of love" (167). Self-reflexivity, Barth suggests, is not finally the refutation, but the condition of that possibility.

Metafiction is all about connection, not solipsism. To read it as autonomous is to read it with realist assumptions, which is, to understand self-reference in terms of precisely the stable dualism of form and content it repudiates. If content is the end of fiction, then to treat form as content is necessarily to internalize this end. But form and content are always producing a tertium quid which, on the contrary, necessarily leads beyond the fiction.

Innovative forms in general should not be perceived as marginal or deviant, but as explorations of the vast range of textual strategies left largely untouched by the dominance of realism in the literary tradition. Among these diverse approaches are many with a capacity to engage reality in ways inaccessible to realist fiction, and innovative fiction should be credited with this potential. Critical attention should not be confined to its formal qualities, as if these were subject enough; nor should it bewail its unrealistic content, as if this would disqualify it from any claim to significance whatever. Innovative fiction does not abandon the conventions of realist representation out of adolescent posturing, glib nihilism or sheer frivolity, but the better to pursue something else: an *argument*. And it is this, the articulated encounter between the creative imagination and the world, that constitutes the proper object of critical attention. It is not to be understood as a reductive abstract, but permeates the whole, polysemous and multifaceted. Nor is it cold or detached: where realist fiction projects emotional force through empathy with its characters, innovative fiction is equally capable of a pathos evoked not vicariously but directly, in the reader's involvement with the argument itself. But this last point, inherently subjective and contingent, is best made in the context of specific readings.

Chapter 2

How to Succeed: Donald Barthelme's
The Dead Father

Donald Barthelme's first novel, *Snow White,* was an analysis of popular culture widely dismissed as a symptom of the malaise it purported to criticize. Because Barthelme's main target in this novel was the debasement of language by which the degraded values of contemporary culture are propagated, and his preferred method was oblique parody, there was always likely to be some uncertainty about his own text's dissociation from its subject. Barthelme's awareness of the problem was apparent in the questionnaire he inserted midway through the novel, which insisted upon the self-consciousness of its manner by eliciting critical responses from its readers.[1] Perhaps some critics found him insufficiently vitriolic in his critique of a culture they themselves held in contempt; but as his metafictional questionnaire indicates, Barthelme is too aware of his own implication in the culture he is writing about to pour immoderate scorn upon it. The novel itself loudly proclaims that "ANATHEMIZATION OF THE WORLD IS NOT AN ADEQUATE RESPONSE TO THE WORLD" (178). For the dwarves, celebrating "dreck" and the "trash phenomenon," this is an alibi for bland acceptance. But for Barthelme himself it implies that his parodic attack upon the prevailing cultural conditions should be qualified by his considerable sympathy for those, Snow White in particular, who are merely its victims.

His stories have been similarly diminished by a tendency among critics to uphold their playfulness as an end in itself. An early popularizing article in the *New York Times Magazine* aggravated this misconception by suggesting that "it is sometimes amusing merely to let his

43

stuff 'wash over you.' "[2] But Barthelme's own comments always resisted such a perception of his work. Against the suggestion that he had not engaged the major social issues of the day—"Vietnam, political scandals, minority rights . . ."—he asserted that "a careful reading of what I've written would disclose that all the things you mention are touched upon. . . . The Vietnam war colored a lot of pieces. It's found in 'The Indian Uprising' and very much in 'Report'. . . ."[3] His method of approaching these issues was indirect, and he was consequently charged with an evasion of straightforward morality. His response to that charge suggests an exploratory rather than expository concept of fiction, by which his achievement in *The Dead Father* might properly be characterized: "It's not the straightforward that's being evaded but the too-true . . . I believe that my every sentence trembles with morality in that each attempts to engage the problematic rather than to present a proposition to which all reasonable men must agree."[4]

The reception of *The Dead Father* by the literary establishment was more than usually mixed—polarized, in fact, between cold dismissal and often immoderate acclaim. Both of these positions seem to stem from largely a priori literary sympathies, and in consequence their arguments seldom engage the text itself in an insightful way; but they do indicate something of the literary issues at stake. The negative responses were all to some degree determined by a perceived failure in Barthelme's novel to fulfil certain basic expectations, expectations which are most clearly apparent in the opinion of Maureen Howard in *Yale Review:* "This cold short narrative is written at an extreme distance from life, out of literary models and the author's idea of a defunct avant-garde."[5] Her objection is that the novel lacks engagement with reality, or "life"; but a distinction has to be drawn between a model of engagement as the work of a novel's argument, which does apply to *The Dead Father,* and a model confined to the narrative subject matter—that is, some concept of realism—which clearly does not. Why the latter should be exclusively valued as a mode of engagement with reality is not clear, but the comment of another reviewer suggests a certain nostalgia for linguistic innocence: "*The Dead Father* presents itself on a larger scale, really as cryptic allegory. But it lacks any sense of jeopardy and urgency. We learn very early

that it is all cardboard."[6] This appears to be a complaint that the novel
fails to engage the reader because it does not create a narrative world
and characters that matter in their own right; but the expectation of
such a vicarious and illusory mode of engagement can hardly be a
convincing literary criterion. If we are told it is all cardboard (which
is not quite true), for this to come as a surprise or a disappointment
suggests a credulous habit of reading that is rather more escapist (and
so presumably further from life, if we are to take the word seriously)
than the alternative offered in *The Dead Father*.

A secondary objection is that the novel is incestuously literary,
more concerned to establish itself in the van of a literary tradition
than to address itself to extra-literary issues—that it is a purely aesthetic object, and therefore estranged from life. Worse still, it is
deemed inadequate even to this model of innovation: "Here may be
found his Lucky speech, his *Watt* palaver, his Joycean flourishes, his
Kafkaesque dream, etc. . . . the awe is still in him and he cannot
bring himself to real parody."[7] The problem of literary influence
used here as an objection to the novel might be better taken as an
enhancement to its argument: achieving autonomy from one's *literary*
fathers is an evident and direct extrapolation from the novel's theme
of fatherhood, and it is logical that this should be manifest in its style.
An example would be the Dead Father's Papsday soliloquy, a Joycean
monologue in which the dominant motifs are relentless punning
(particularly the use of "end" for the en- prefix), the incantatory
use of Latinate phrases, and repetition—the insistent reiteration of
"reiterate," for example. It is not exactly parody, since it does not
function as an implicit critique of the manner or author parodied.
But what exactly would a "real parody" of Joyce consist of? With
language already so self-conscious and ironic, the self-critical function
of parodic language has been largely preempted. This is more mim-
icry than parody, an appropriation of style to a different end, the
nature and rationale of which is the burden of the novel's argument.
Barthelme's formal innovation is not an irresponsible aestheticism,
but the means to a more sophisticated engagement with life. He has
himself said that "the change of emphasis from the what to the how
seems to me to be the major impulse in art since Flaubert, and it's
not merely formalism, it's not at all superficial, it's an attempt to reach

truth, and a very rigorous one. You don't get, following this path, a
moral universe set out in ten propositions, but we already have that."[8]

The enthusiastic reviews competed in allegorical interpretation of
the Dead Father himself, producing long lists of tentative solutions
with the apparent hope that, if none of them seemed adequate alone,
a sufficiently extensive set might capture the novel's meaning. Some
critics, uncomfortable with the text's inconsistency in invoking such
a multiplicity of allegorical significations, sought to order them hier-
archically beneath a single master interpretation. Richard Todd offered a representative list, then moved to a higher level of abstraction:
"He is God first of all. . . . After that he's what you will: The novel,
Western Culture, Truth, Duty, Honor, Country. He is the order that
we seek, and the control we seek to escape."[9] This is nice in that it
epigrammatizes the ambivalence with which the Dead Father is
viewed, but it is also a long way removed from the page-by-page text
of the novel. It is not that such an allegorical meaning is invalid, but
that having been chosen, it imposes a logic upon the text that distorts
or neglects its literal development. In other words, while it is clear
that the literal sense is not of great consequence on its own (just as
the vehicle of a metaphor is inconsequential except in its metaphoric
function), this literal narrative rather than its "translation" must remain the centre of attention if the exploratory process it facilitates is
not to be subverted by a prejudicial allegorical framework. The idea
of fatherhood is a more fundamental unifying principle in *The Dead
Father* than any abstract allegorical formulation.

Support for such an interpretative emphasis is also available in
Barthelme's own comments on the novel. Asked to explain the
germinating idea for *The Dead Father,* he replied simply, "A matter of
having a father and being a father."[10] This remark must be taken as
rather disingenuous and insufficient grounds on its own for inferring
authorial intention, but he was a little more expansive in another
interview: "*The Dead Father* suggests that the process of becoming has
bound up in it the experience of many other consciousnesses, the
most important of which are in a law-giving relation to the self.
The characters complain about this in what I hope is an interesting
fashion."[11] The emphasis here remains upon essentially filial subjectivity, without excluding the (social, theological, political) analogues

upon which the scenario impinges. It is clear, though, that these latter
are derivative from the literal sense of paternity in the novel, not
hidden codes that provide its driving force. The singular parallelism
of simple allegory is inadequate to *The Dead Father* because no single
interpretation satisfies; nor does it evoke any set of allegorical meanings with sufficient consistency to justify reading it as a multiple
allegory. As with Kafka, whose paternity is apparent at more than
one point in Barthelme's novel, the blunt dualism of allegory ultimately fails to account for the degree to which the literal sense
generates the narrative. It is not allegorical parallelism that should be
the centre of critical attention, then, but the framework upon which
the novel itself constructs its argument, the question of fatherhood.
In it Barthelme has found his unifying master-theme, one which can
be used not as an abstract thesis but as an open metaphor: a metaphor
whose tenor is unspecified and unfixed while its vehicle is developed
on its own terms, according to its own logic, and becomes in the
process a vehicle of discovery.

The opening tableau of *The Dead Father,* in which his huge body
is described lying prostrate across the city, is formally separate from
the narrative that follows; it lacks a chapter number and is printed in
italic type. It stands in relation to the rest of the text as the condition
upon which its action is predicated, a sort of protasis, the Dead
Father's enormous impassive presence in the city reminiscent of the
situation in Barthelme's earlier story, "The Balloon."[12] Unlike the
balloon, the Dead Father has not appeared one night, but preexists
the earliest memories of the citizens; he is a constant, colouring the
whole of their experience. The essential fact here is the overbearing
timelessness of his presence, which is also expressed in the static
structure of the piece, a formal description of the Dead Father (head,
body, left leg, right leg) in which the effect upon the lives of the
citizens appears only parenthetically. The description is matter-of-fact
in tone while repeatedly nodding in the direction of the epic narrative
the Dead Father himself would demand, admitting in this ironic
stance the double-edged mythic dimension of the Dead Father: myth
as both past and powerfully present, awesome yet ludicrously anachronistic. So, the Dead Father is granted the heroic attributes he is
due, but they are presented less as archetypes than as clichés: "The

brow is noble, good Christ, what else? Broad and noble. And serene, of course, he's dead, what else if not serene?" and "Jawline compares favorably to a rock formation. Imposing, rugged, all that."[13]

The novel works continually to keep open the broader intimations of its argument, and the essential statement of its fundamental premise is given devoid of specific context, isolated in a single line paragraph: "Dead, but still with us, still with us, but dead" (3). That this is an unsatisfactory state of affairs, and that nothing is being done about it, is the motivation for the expedition that follows. In their impotence, the citizens remain children. The problem for Thomas, in undertaking to dispose of the Dead Father, is that he must to some extent become him.

In the first chapter this process is already under way, with Thomas at the head of the expedition that will drag the Dead Father to his grave. What is at stake in the confrontation between these two is illustrated by their contrasting ideas of authority. In the case of the Dead Father, this is manifest in his long-standing imposition upon his sons of a humiliating uniform of cap-and-bells, "for the good of all," according to the paternalistic refrain that echoes from the protasis onward. Juxtaposed with this is an example of Thomas's leadership, his recruitment to the expedition of the drunk, Edmund, against his better judgement: "It would be the making of him, he said. Our march. I did not agree. But it is hard to deny someone the thing he thinks will be the making of him. I signed him up" (7). In an absurd way Edmund's belief proves correct: the Dead Father unpredictably makes him his heir (166). But this outcome is not necessary to the contrast between the Dead Father's and Thomas's ideas of benevolent authority, the one abstract and formal, "A matter of Organization" (7), and the other intimately informed by the needs of its subjects.

Thomas's attempt to establish a new mode of authority is constantly undermined by the allure of the old order, however, and the resulting ambivalence colours both the abstract issue of forms of authority and the relationship between Thomas and the Dead Father himself. A quasi-psychoanalytical explanation of this ambivalence is provided by Julie, in her whimsical narrative of the onset of fatherhood: "The fucked mother conceives, Julie said. The whelpling is, after agonies I shall not describe, whelped. Then the dialogue begins.

The father speaks to it. The 'it' in a paroxysm of not understanding. The 'it' whirling as in a centrifuge. Looking for something to tie to. Like a boat in a storm. What is there? The father" (77). The father is both the threatening other who generates difference (by speaking to the child) and the only possible means by which this experience can be assimilated. This primal scene has a fundamental relation to the problem of language: the father, in the very act of attempting to communicate, initiates the disjunction between self and other that makes it necessary and impossible. The gap is generated by the language that seeks to close it. The child is therefore confronted with the choice between language, which forever guarantees that gap in the impassable barrier between signifier and signified, or acceptance of the father as origin, the authority in which signifier and signified are unified and by that tautology, the theological "I AM," the arbiter of truth. The child chooses the latter. The father, then, offers both hostility and security, the impossibility and condition of meaning. Of course to put it in this way is simply to juggle the buzzwords of Lacanian psychoanalysis, risking a substitution of jargon for values that is avoided by Barthelme. It is a tendency he satirized in "A Shower of Gold,"[14] where the subject was existentialism, or rather its popular degradation; but as he explains in an interview, "You could do the same story today and substitute the current vocabulary and very little of the structure of the story would have to be changed. Call it 'The Lacanthrope.' "[15] Barthelme's allusions to Lacan are too light and fanciful to risk any leaden incantation of his themes, or any uncritical acceptance of his narrative's validity. Julie speaks in the context of a parlour game of intellectual disputation—"Fatherhood as a substructure of the war of all against all, said Thomas, we could discuss that" (76)—and it is the idiosyncrasy of her own conceptual language that dominates.

The effort to escape the domination of the father, then, is always undercut by the lack of a structure outside that which he dominates. To move beyond this is to embrace uncertainty and insecurity. This ambivalence is not only apparent in the original relationship of fatherhood, but also in the higher structures in which its formula is repeated. So, in terms of patriarchal sexual politics, the insidious attraction of the old order, the nostalgia for its security felt even by its

antagonists is explored through Emma's near capitulation to the Dead
Father's advances. Though resolutely antipatriarchal elsewhere, she is
powerfully drawn by the comfortable prefeminist domesticity that
the Dead Father implicitly offers her. She manifests a longing for a
role that allows her, at the price of her autonomy, the luxuries of an
irresponsible passivity: she is vulnerable to the flattery of the chival-
rous courtship enacted (or travestied) by the Dead Father, and she
muses nostalgically on the petty pleasures of the middle-class housewife—distraught particularly at the waste of her domestic talent for
making salads. Ultimately, however, she refuses the Dead Father—
politely, even tenderly, and certainly with regret:

> Come to bed, dear salad-head. Come to bed with me.
> No I won't, said Emma. Pardon me for saying it but you are,
> you are, you are too old. (97)

Dead, in fact: but the translation of that absolute into relative terms
testifies to the impossibility of simply repudiating an order so intrinsic
to our own being, and so seductive of our anxieties.

Bound up with the rejection of the old order are the *grounds* for
Oedipal or generational rebellion, the problem of the evaluative
criteria for the new. Julie, like Snow White in Barthelme's first novel,
is driven by ennui to a desire for the new as such, a value in itself. An
undiscriminating appetite for the new is a contemporary malaise
which has preoccupied Barthelme elsewhere; in "The Flight of the
Pigeons from the Palace,"[16] for example, where its consequences in
art are explored. The fact that Barthelme's own innovative fictions
cater to this desire indicates his considerable sympathy, but he is also
conscious of the need to espouse a value beyond mere newness. In
the *Paris Review* interview he explains the inadequacy of the criterion
of newness with reference to a story in *Great Days:* "Reynolds Price
in the *Times* said of my story 'The New Music' that it was about as
new as the toothache. He apparently didn't get the joke, which is
that there is always a new music—the new music shows up about
every ten minutes. Not like the toothache. More like hiccups." But
he also offers an interpretation of its underlying motivation: "It
equates with being able to feel something rather than with novelty
per se, it's a kind of shorthand for discovery."[17] Julie's uncritical

desire for the new in *The Dead Father* is gratified, on the occasion of
the big dance, by the arrival of a group of apes. She dances with one
and attempts conversation:

> Can you talk at all?
> (Silence)
> Nothing?
> (Silence)
> That's new. (101)

She is forced to maintain a breathless monologue to fill the silence—
"I had my work cut out for me just keeping the conversation going," she later tells Thomas (103)—and the point is made. But the
conversation with Thomas continues in the same animated manner,
in sharp contrast to the curt exchanges before the apes' arrival; indirectly, an affective discovery has indeed been made, and Emma
concludes the chapter, "This is the best dance I have ever been to!"
(104).

While the Dead Father stands above all for the permanence of his
power, then, he is confronted with an antithetical view which, insisting upon change as a value, negates him utterly. Against his own
concept of his seniority as authority, Julie advances her view of him
as "an old fart" (10), triggering a reflex response that the same phrase,
the refutation of paternal authority, will produce twice more in the
novel: the Dead Father storms off, and is discovered "slaying" in a
grove of musicians. An extravagant list of the slain is given, the
linguistic foregrounding of which prepares for the textual trump by
which Julie shrivels his achievement: "Impressive, said Julie, had they
not been pure cardboard" (12). By breaking the language contract
guaranteeing the father's authority, the primacy of language is here
exploited to counter the very physical but contingent power wielded
by the Dead Father. The change of label for the Dead Father's victims
from "musicians" to "artists" in this passage suggests a confrontation
between art and authority (music is Barthelme's favoured representative art form, as in "The New Music").[18] But the victory is not so
unequivocal, and language not so uncompromised. When the theme
of art arises again, this time in terms of the visual arts, the Dead
Father's control is absolute:

Tell me, said Julie, did you ever want to paint or draw or etch?
Yourself?

It was not necessary, said the Dead Father, because I am the
Father. All lines my lines. All figure and all ground mine, out of
my head. All colors mine. You take my meaning.

We had no choice, said Julie. (19)

As Julie's response makes clear, the implication is that language remains an inheritance contaminated by its past. It is no more possible
to disown completely the meaning endowed upon it by the father
than it is to disown the structure of fatherhood itself. The way
language is used in *The Dead Father* itself, then, is of fundamental
importance to its argument.

The narrative proper begins *in medias res,* proceeding ahead of the
world that may be inferred from it, rather than presenting itself as the
animation of a landscape already set out in words (which latter
procedure is effectively how the novel works in terms of thematic
preoccupation, developing out of the protasis). Since in this novel the
imperative to construct a world "behind" the words is secondary,
contingent upon the argument of the text, there is no necessary
consistency between the requirements of the latter and the expectations normally brought to the former. In the case of such anomalies
as a talking dead father these expectations must be abandoned completely—"dead," it must be accepted, means "dead only in a sense"
(14). In allegorical terms this would mean establishing a metaphorical
death (the death of God, the novel, patriarchal society; the superses-
sion of objective truth, moral law, ego-psychology) that is in some
way incomplete. To remain more closely engaged with the text, it
involves the conclusion that the power and presence embodied in
fatherhood is a function of the experience of it, is in fact an aspect of
experience wholly independent of the physical body in which it is
incarnate. So that the ambiguous nature of the expedition as either a
rejuvenating quest for the "Golden Fleece," or the funeral march it
turns out to be, is one of the survival or disposal of the *experience* of
paternity that was (is) the Dead Father.

The argument cannot be conducted in a vacuum, however, and
the resultant tension between the need to contain a suspect language
and the need for a representational context is made explicit by Bar-

thelme's inclusion of three diagrams in the text to perform the contextual function. Theoretically, these are better suited to the task than language, whose indeterminate connotations tend always to say more than is required, to upset the desired emphasis. Their presence in the text testifies to the nature of this emphasis, but also demonstrates their own inadequacy to it. The first is a diagram of the seating arrangements for a lunch of toasted prawns shared by the Dead Father, Thomas and Julie, and falls victim to its diagrammatic method: the tablecloth is square, and so the fourth place around its edge is filled, illogically but neatly, by the prawns themselves. Offered as a more exact means of representation than language, the diagram proves at least as unwieldy. In the same way the second diagram, an aerial view of the line of march, invites comparison with the language for which it is substituted. Here too the diagram, like language, cannot avoid specifying too much, imposing too rigid a structure upon the loose formation it attempts to convey, and so implying too much meaning, presenting the incidental as significant. The third diagram recalls the first, this time a round tablecloth and four persons. But here the diagram provokes disharmonious inferences of hierarchy among the diners, which are based (since the tablecloth is round) purely upon its orientation on the page. The most elementary fact of the medium here ensures its representational inadequacy (or superfluity).

This problematic tension is incorporated into the form of the novel in the continuous conflict it enacts between the need to describe in the interests of the narrative, and its resistance to representational criteria: "They packed up. Thomas gave the signal. The cable jerked. The sun still. Trees. Vegetation. Wild gooseberries. Weather" (9). Such gestural travesties of rendition indicate a significant dissent from the normal novelistic focus of interest. The burden of significance in the novel is carried almost entirely in dialogue and monologue, in language attributable to or indicative of a particular subjectivity. The narrative world is a shadow cast by language, ontologically posterior rather than prior to it, and while it is coherently articulated (it is a narrative) it implies no coherence in those of its aspects that are not specified. The Dead Father is explicitly 3,200 cubits long, but his behaviour and treatment in the narrative would often require the inference (if it were to be made) that he is human in scale. The inference is not to be made, because this contradiction is simply an implicit by-product of language that addresses other issues.

There are several points in the novel where a requirement for contextual detail is met by an absurd and bizarre list: the slain musicians, the items fathered by the Dead Father, the slain animals, the qualities of the two hotels, the inventory of the Dead Father's estate, the shopping list. These resist the purposive assumptions by which we normally read literature, for while they perform the general task of aiding verisimilitude in their form, they deny it in their content. Yet they are not pointed enough for parody, nor do they offer themselves for any other signifying purpose. On such criteria these lists must be judged arbitrary; but since the narrative of the novel accepts in its form the necessity of rendition without the constraint of realist conventions, the detail by which this is achieved is intrinsically undermotivated. If the detail is arbitrary, it is necessarily so: Barthelme chooses to emphasize the fact, testing the range of unfettered imagination in such a way that the representational function of these lists is itself enlisted in the service of his argument. Language is used as a means of outgrowing the structure within which it remains inscribed, as an instance of the ambivalent relationship that structures the novel itself. The need for narrative rendition is accepted, but its tendency towards realism is subverted in the particularity of the language used—just as Thomas accepts the structure of paternity but works within it to minimize its authoritarianism.

The boldest use of language in the novel is the series of almost abstract dialogues between Julie and Emma, which stretches meaning to its breaking point. The dialogues offer, as a narrative mode, an alternative to the Dead Father as origin of meaning; as such they stand in parallel with several other models of fatherlessness that are offered in the course of the expedition, all of which are compromised. The first of these is provided by two children, both aged ten, in love. Their attitude towards the Dead Father shows a naive-utopian freedom from the thrall of his authority, but it is an inadequate model because it is utterly private, unable to survive exposure to society at large: "We are going to live together all our lives and love each other all our lives until we die. We know it. But don't tell anyone because we'll be beaten, if the knowledge becomes general" (14). The Wends, through whose country the party passes, are another model of society free from the thrall of paternity: "We Wends are the fathers of ourselves . . . that which all men have wished to be, from the very beginning, we are" (73). But this model too is utopian, and unavailable: "The mechanics of the thing elude me, said Thomas" (73). In a book that centres obsessively upon the male lineage of fathers and sons, patriarchy and paternity, particular significance hangs upon the fact that its most radical set-piece dialogues occur exclusively between the novel's two principal female characters. They constitute another model of fatherlessness, of nonpatriarchal society: an anarchist-feminist enclave within the narrative of the expedition, in which Emma functions as a foil to Julie, who is established throughout the book as the antithesis of the Dead Father and the principal advocate of the chaos of fatherlessness that Thomas must balance against the Dead Father's authority.

Introduced as "conversation," the dialogues are verbal collages in which neither speaker is bound by the context of the previous locution. The speeches are not attributed, and as the dialogues progress confusion about who is speaking is propagated by the shift of motifs from one to the other. There is, at least in the first dialogue, a basic thread of contextual sense: Julie is hostile towards Emma and seeking to get rid of her; Emma is curious, especially about Thomas, and intent upon staying. But they are dominated by the effects of repetition and juxtaposition of various enigmatic phrases, some of which have an apparent relevance to the dialogues themselves— "Hoping this will reach you at a favorable moment" (23, 24, 86, 155); or to the narrative context—"I can make it hot for you" (24, 25, 26, 61, 150); but often they suggest no relevance whatever— "Thought I heard a dog barking" (25, 26, 26, 62, 86, 148). Such an approach involves a treatment of language that tends to disregard its referential function. Barthelme does not consider himself to be working in this way, but does acknowledge its attraction: "There's an urge towards abstraction that's very seductive . . . the sort of thing you find in Gertrude Stein and hardly anywhere else."[19] In fact the movement towards treating language as abstract, far from obscuring its referentiality, serves only to highlight it. In these dialogues every speech introduces new deictic implications so diverse and in such rapid succession, with scarcely any consolidation of reference from one to the next, that the effect is not an appreciation of language as music but an exasperated reaching after meaning. Although recognizable aesthetic criteria are at work in the incantatory repetitions and thematic recurrence to certain lexical fields, they do not usurp the sense of intent inherent in the referentiality of language. As a refusal of coherence rather than an alternative to it, the dialogues fail to establish an independent value structure and remain subordinate to the intentionality they defy.

This intentionality remains the centre of interest, and compelling effects are achieved by the slightest suggestions of sense that emerge from such unpropitious circumstances. Such effects are only possible against the background of a well-defined narrative context—the short stories Barthelme has written in this form, notably in *Great Days,* are far less radical in their disruptions. In particular, the situations of Julie and Emma in the narrative are a fundamental premise. In the third dialogue a particularly disorientating effect is achieved and gradually resolved by the slow realization (made possible by a degree of consistency in the preferred catch-phrases of either speaker) that in this instance it was Emma, not Julie, who spoke first. That such a switch is discernible at all reinforces the sense of a meaning trembling just beyond the reader's comprehension, an effect of exclusion which is enhanced at those points where the exchanges suddenly briefly cohere, and the dialogists appear to understand each other on a basis which remains wholly mysterious to the reader:

> This idiot had led a thoroughly disorderly life.
> Sorry to hear that.
> Covered with butter.
> Chocolate butter?
> Yes chocolate butter. (88)

The dialogues get progressively longer through the book, achieving their effects on an increasingly large scale against the background of better defined reader expectation. The process of reading them is one of constantly delayed resolution, more and more material being held in suspension against the possibility of retrospective coherence.

This is of course never provided, but there are occasions on which the process is stimulated, when a phrase that has already occurred without identifiable context reoccurs in an exchange where it achieves sudden coherence. But to go back to previous instances of the phrase armed with this insight is to learn little or nothing—the effect of resolution is wholly aesthetic. Ultimately the dislocations of meaning introduce into the interpretative act an irreducible element of play, the pursuit of meaning liberated from any expectations of resolution. The reader is beckoned along semantic trails which do not end or meet (though they may cross) but are simply abandoned in the proliferation of alternatives. What is denied is the end-directed, the definitive and the singular in meaning, in favour of the exploratory, speculative and polysemous. But in the process the imperative to order, which remains of importance to Thomas, is completely abandoned.

As such, these dialogues stand in clear contrast to the monolithic epic narrative with which the Dead Father makes his claim to authority. Related as he is being dragged along, the Dead Father's narrative is a parody of several heroic conventions—catalogues of gifts and offspring, cunning disguises, descent into the underworld, intrepid escapes—and its message is singular and direct: that its protagonist (the Dead Father) is the hero. A comparable tautology is his pyrotechnic speech to the men, where in reply to Emma's enquiry as to its meaning, the Dead Father says "it meant I made a speech" (51). The women respond sarcastically to the Dead Father's assertion of patriarchal authority, and go on to envision feminist alternative worlds, hypothesizing the inversion of patriarchy or, more radically, a break with the whole structure of that power relationship:

> It is obvious that but for a twist of fate we and not they would be calling the tune, said Julie.
> It is obvious that but for a twist of fate the mode of the music would be different, said Emma. Much different. (39)

Given the analogy of music and art in general that is already established in the novel and elsewhere in Barthelme's fiction, the use of the metaphor here leads directly back to the contrast between the Dead Father's phallic narrative and the elusive dialogues of the women. These are certainly a different mode of music; but they remain, within the terms of the novel, estranged from the central action, marginalized by their failure to coordinate their escape from the patriarchal linear narrative with the evolution of a functional alternative structure of signification; another compromised model of fatherlessness.

The narrative offered by Thomas in response to the Dead Father's does not repeat the narrator-as-hero model, but rather presents him as a Kafkaesque victim: "One day in a wild place far from the city four men in dark suits with shirts and ties and attaché cases containing Uzi submachine guns seized me, saying that I was wrong and had always been wrong and would always be wrong and that they were not going to hurt me. Then they hurt me, first with can openers then with corkscrews" (40). It is a narrative of the psychology of sons, ending in confrontation with the phallic Great Father Serpent. To the riddle this monster poses, "What do you really feel?" Thomas gives the correct reply (which he has read, not felt), "like murder-inging"—and is surprised at how well this articulates his suppressed Oedipal desires: "I myself wondered, and marveled, but what I was wondering and marveling at was the closeness with which what I had answered accorded with my feelings, my lost feelings that I had never found before" (46). He is left "with murderinging in mind—the dream of a stutterer" (46). The felicity of this would appear to be sufficient cause of the extra "ing," both in respect of the concatenation of "murder" and "ringing," and Thomas's later admission "when I explain myself I tend to stutter" (56), though its initial effect is principally as a cautionary supererogation of sense. The Dead Father, recognizing the pertinence of the tale to himself, is disconcerted, and seeks to undermine the authority of the narrative. Thomas's reply changes the rules upon which the objection is based and shifts the burden of authority onto the act of interpretation, a trap into which the Dead Father unhesitatingly falls:

That is a tall tale, said the Dead Father. I don't believe it ever happened.
No tale ever happened in the way we tell it, said Thomas, but the moral is always correct.

What is the moral?

Murderinging, Thomas said.

Murderinging is not correct, said the Dead Father. The sacred and noble Father should not be murdereded. Never. Absolutely not.

I mentioned no names, said Thomas. (46)

The Dead Father has been flustered into acknowledging the particular significance of the moral to himself, and the breakthrough is followed by the first of a series of symbolic transfers of power that occur at key stages through the novel: silver buckle, sword, passport, keys.

The shape of the novel is determined by Thomas's efforts to complete the transfer of power without in the process becoming the image of the Dead Father; the crucial issue being whether it is possible to usurp the Dead Father's position without also taking on his monolithic perspective. The balance is very fine between transformation and repetition in Thomas's appropriation to himself of the role of father; he is seduced by some of its rewards, notably the pleasure of control, into a dangerous proximity with the position represented by the Dead Father. The significant difference, however, is that when confronted Thomas does not attempt a mystification of the role of fatherhood but frankly confesses its attractions, while the Dead Father's preferred policy is an obfuscation of the nature of power relations:

> I *like* telling everybody what to do, Thomas said. It is a great pleasure, being boss. One of the greatest. Wouldn't you agree? he said to the Dead Father.
>
> It is one of the best pleasures, the Dead Father said. No doubt about it. It is bang-up, but mostly we don't let people know. Mostly we downplay the pleasure. Mostly we stress the anguish. We keep the pleasure to ourselves, in our hearts. Occasionally we may show a bit of it to someone—lift a corner of the veil, as it were. But we only do that in order to certify the pleasure to ourselves. Full disclosure is almost unheard of. Thomas is being criminally frank, in my opinion. (66)

Part of Thomas's approach to the problem of authority is this process of "full disclosure," a laying bare of the motives and grounds that

form a self-conscious attempt to retain around the process the qualify-
ing frame of its contingency and answerability. So Thomas counters
the Dead Father's assertion of his larger perspective by claiming a
greater understanding of the limits of perspective, limits the Dead
Father would rather not acknowledge:

> My criticism was that you never understood the larger picture,
> said the Dead Father. Young men never understand the larger
> picture.
> I don't suggest I understand it now. I do understand the frame.
> The limits.
> Of course the frame is easier to understand.
> Older people tend to overlook the frame, even when they are
> looking right at it, said Thomas. They don't like to think about it.
> (32)

The Dead Father's reluctance to acknowledge the frame is his reluctance to acknowledge his own death, his attempt to impose upon the
structure he dominates a timeless universality. On the other hand,
Thomas's emphasis on the frame receives some modification at the
hands of Julie. When she proclaims their unity, Thomas angers her
by insisting upon seeing this in the context of mutability, and so
declaring it temporary: his emphasis on the temporal frame here leads
to a devaluation of the present, an abdication from involvement. Julie
affects a reconciliation in sex, but exacts a succinct and didactic
revenge that reasserts the primacy of the present:

> Julie made a circle of thumb and forefinger and popped him
> smartly on the ball.
> Anguish of Thomas.
> It will pass, she said, dearly beloved, it is only temporary. (69)

Thomas demonstrates that he has assimilated Julie's teachings when
he is called upon to allay the doubts of the men—"*are we doing the
right thing?*" (92)—about the expedition. He relates an anecdote in
which Haydn refuses Martin Luther's telephone request that he "do
a piece for *us*" (93), to which Edmund reasonably objects "You have
got the centuries all wrong and the telephone should not be in there
and anyway I do not get the point" (93). Thomas's answer is inviting

as a central statement of the context within which moral engagement is placed in the novel, and in Barthelme's work as a whole. There is no abdication of responsibility here, but rather a heightening of it through an unswerving consciousness of the uncertain context in which it must operate: "You see! Thomas exclaimed. *There it is!* Things are not simple. Error is always possible, even with the best intentions in the world. People make mistakes. Things are not done right. Right things are not done. There are cases which are not clear. You must be able to tolerate the anxiety. To do otherwise is to jump ship, ethics-wise" (93). This is Thomas's awareness of the frame integrated into a commitment to action, rather than as a pretext for passivity. Its imperative to engagement is set in relief by the negative response of the alcoholic Edmund: "I hate anxiety, Edmund said. He produced a flask and tilted it" (93).

The question of the structure in which action is to be located is addressed by the "Manual for Sons," which takes the novel's argument to its crisis. The manual deals with the father-son relationship in diverse aspects, offering advice that assumes the normal power structure of that relationship in a tone (that of a manual for parents) that inverts it. Some of the sections, such as "Dandling" and "Sexual organs," appear to address themselves to fathers rather than sons, both of these offering advice on the niceties of a father's sexuality in relation to his children, daughters in particular. This anticipates the manual's conclusions on the transfer of paternal power, the central issue of Thomas's situation. The problem is not one of killing the father—"time will slay him, that is a virtual certainty" (145)—but of liberation from his influence. Death is never the end of the father's authority: "Fatherless now, you must deal with the memory of a father. Often that memory is more potent than the living presence of a father, is an inner voice commanding, haranguing, yes-ing and no-ing. . . . At what point do you become yourself? Never, wholly, you are always partly him. That privileged position in your inner ear is his last 'perk' and no father has ever passed it by" (144). The manual's conclusion, then, is that the inherited role of fatherhood is realistically not to be abandoned but rather ameliorated: "Your true task, as a son, is to reproduce every one of the enormities touched upon in this manual, but in attenuated form. You must become your father, but a paler, weaker version of him. The enormities go with the job, but close study will allow you to perform the job less well than it has previously been done, thus moving towards a golden age of decency, quiet and calmed fevers" (145). The manual's programme of reform is moderate rather than radical, not through choice but because it accepts the taint of inherited structure (psychological, conceptual, social, economic, political, aesthetic) as a necessary condition of subsequent action. The reception of the book by Julie and Thomas provides a measure of their respective positions on the question of fatherhood. They are unable to decide whether the book is too harsh or not harsh enough, an indeterminacy for which Thomas provides a rationalization deeply unsatisfactory to Julie:

> It would depend on the experience of the individual making the judgement, as to whether it was judged to be too harsh or judged to be not harsh enough.
> I hate relativists, she said, and threw the book into the fire. (146)

That Julie's anger is directed at the book rather than at Thomas indicates a parallelism between the problem of its evaluation and the problem it addresses. Julie is caught between her desire for an absolute solution and her inability to provide one (the felt oppression of fatherhood and the anarchy of fatherlessness), while Thomas's pragmatic relativism aligns him with the manual's conclusions.

The success of the novel depends upon more than the resolution of its argument, however. How does such a narrative engage the interest and especially the sympathies of the reader? Certainly, little is offered in terms of involvement with the characters—in fact this is actively discouraged. Barthelme's commitment is to a narrative technique incompatible with the complex rendering of character needed to achieve this sort of emotional effect. He has himself identified the tendency of his writing to defuse emotion with humour. There is certainly a great deal of humour in *The Dead Father*, but the novel also appeals to the emotions, by providing a very strong affective focus at a higher level. The effect of the novel's ending does not depend upon any emotional identification with the characters, who even by that stage have a functional rather than an individual status—

the Dead Father in particular, though his demise is the centre of reader involvement. This affective involvement is in fact only locatable in terms of the novel's argument: it does not attach to the Dead Father as such, but to the multiple ambivalences that have accumulated around him. The argument of the novel must be understood to involve more than the analytical exploration of a set of related themes that a nonfictional treatment might have produced. It is a means of establishing and developing the several perspectives from which the reader may recognize, and be affected by, the pertinence of its material; it is an arena for the reciprocity of interpretation and affective response. Even when the characters in a novel are meant to matter in their own right, our involvement can be understood in these terms. But the nature of a novel's importance to us is perhaps clearer, and our engagement with it more active, when it is not mediated through a vicarious dramatis personae. The final chapter brings The Dead Father to his grave, a great hole in the ground, and to a subdued recognition of his fate: "The Dead Father looked again at the hole. Oh, he said, I see" (174). He is relieved of his sustaining myth, the rejuvenating Golden Fleece:

> No Fleece? asked the Dead Father.
> Thomas looked at Julie.
> She has it?
> Julie lifted her skirt.
> Quite golden, said the Dead Father. Quite ample. That's it?
> All there is, Julie said. Unfortunately. But this much. This is where life lives. A pretty problem. As mine as yours. I'm sorry. (174–5)

Julie's pubis *is* the seat of rejuvenation, but no stay against time and change. There is continuity of structure, but it is fluid, not the ossified hierarchy to which the Dead Father clings. He climbs into the hole, his dignity greatest at his end. This is no gleeful conquest, and the representatives of a new and finally ascendant order cannot but mingle admiration with their rejection of the old:

> I'm in it now, said the Dead Father, resonantly.
> What a voice, said Julie, I wonder how he does it.
> She knelt and clasped a hand.

Intolerable, Thomas said. Grand. I wonder how he does it.
I'm in the hole now, said the Dead Father.
Julie holding a hand.
One moment more! said the Dead Father.
Bulldozers. (176–7)

Chapter 3

"A Man's Story Is His Gris-Gris": Cultural Slavery, Literary Emancipation and Ishmael Reed's *Flight to Canada*

Ishmael Reed's early novels appeared in a context that made literary disengagement unthinkable: that of African-American writing in the civil rights turmoil of the sixties. Yet they were strikingly innovative works; for Reed, this innovation was not only *not* an evasion of reality, it was in itself politically affirmative. With the emergence of black nationalism late in the decade, the delineation of a new black aesthetic had become an urgent issue. It was first and most persistently raised by Hoyt Fuller in *Negro Digest,* and soon became the staple of radical black little magazines across America. In 1971 the appearance of a collection of essays entitled *The Black Aesthetic,* and edited by Addison Gayle, brought some coherence to the debate—and sanctified its assumptions.[1] In his own contributions to that book, Gayle recorded the passing of the myth of the American melting pot and the consequent need to repudiate assimilationism. He argued that black nationalism implied the development of a black aesthetic in direct opposition to prevailing aesthetic criteria, in which white cultural concerns were privileged under a guise of "universalism": this bogus universalism was actually the marginalization of black perspectives and black writers by a white literary establishment. Such observations established the need for a new black aesthetic, and prescriptions for its form proliferated. These blueprints were set down at a rapid series of conferences, where black writers past and present were tried against the new criteria. The emergent consensus was for writing that directly recreated the black experience out of which it arose; that found its style in the forms of "black folk expression"; that

was socially progressive in effect—according to a very literal, functional concept of literature; that addressed itself to the common
readership of black people; and that assiduously cultivated positive
black characters.

Reed was one of the few young black writers willing to confront
this prescriptive agenda, dismissing it as a "goon squad aesthetic,"[2] and
explicitly repudiating it in his own writing. While sharing the opposition of the black aesthetic critics to the hegemony of white culture, he
considered their narrow prescriptions to consolidate the marginalization of black writing as simply protest literature. Such a rigidly defined
black aesthetic, he argued, merely confirmed the white liberal establishment's sub-literary expectations of African-American writing.
Black writing should be free to explore its own cultural sources and
define its own forms, that act itself being the affirmation of a black aesthetic. Reed consequently drew criticism from Gayle for the supposed
frivolity and dangerous mythologizing of his novels. He was condemned by both Gayle and Houston Baker for his negative, satirical
treatment of black characters other than the universally reviled "Uncle
Tom" figure. Most fundamentally, his rejection of realism was stigmatized as escapism and a neglect of his responsibility to provide for reader
identification in a common ground of black experience. But more significantly, these considerations also set Reed against Amiri Baraka, the
literary hero of black nationalism and one of its most outspoken theo-
rists; and when Baraka himself came to repudiate nationalism, his criticism of Reed became even more implacable. To Baraka, whose concept of the black aesthetic had now been recast in revolutionary
socialist terms, Reed's neglect of the issue of capitalist exploitation and
his individualist stance revealed him as a middle-class capitulationist, an
archetypal Uncle Tom.

The confrontation between Reed and his black critics was first
played out in his early novel *Yellow Back Radio Broke-Down* (1969).
Its cowboy hero Loop Garoo is confronted by Bo Shmo and his
"neo-social realist gang," who charge that "your work is a blur and
a doodle." Loop's reply encapsulates Reed's rebellion against the
constraints upon the African-American literary tradition: "What's
your beef with me Bo Shmo, what if I write circuses? No one says a
novel has to be one thing. It can be anything it wants to be, a

vaudeville show, the six o' clock news, the mumblings of wild men saddled by demons."[3] The peculiar interest of *Flight to Canada* among Reed's novels is its return to the subject matter of the archetype of African-American fiction, the slave narrative. He had renounced the conventions of this form in his first novel, *The Free-Lance Pallbearers* (1967), "a parody of the confessional mode which is the fundamental, undergirding convention of African-American narrative."[4] His refusal of this tradition opened the way for Reed to elaborate an alternative in his subsequent novels, the "Voodoo aesthetic" he advanced as a more authentic model of the African-American cultural heritage. This project extends through *Yellow Back Radio Broke-Down, Mumbo Jumbo* (1972) and *The Last Days of Louisiana Red* (1974), until in *Flight to Canada* he was able to return and reappropriate the slave narrative on his own terms. Reed's slave narrative does not follow the simple linear form, that of the protagonist's difficult progress towards freedom from a condition of slavery, by which the genre is conventionally structured. Rather, he divides his attention between the experiences of two principal characters: the fugitive Quickskill, and Uncle Robin, the slave who remains behind on the master's plantation (in accordance with the model of *Uncle Tom's Cabin*). He uses this opposition to develop a two-pronged argument about the true nature of emancipation and the means by which it is to be obtained, and this argument is enriched by a metaphorical interpretation of slavery which anchors it firmly to a contemporary frame of reference.

This metaphorical dimension, the focus of narrative attention upon the present as much as on the period of the action, is proclaimed by one of the book's most pervasive comic devices, the use of anachronism. It is already implicit in the novel's punning title, and combines two distinct aspects: it creates a contemporary atmosphere through the casual use of props such as jumbo jets, telephones, satellite television, *Time* magazine, *New York Review of Books,* and all the paraphernalia of contemporary civilization; it also involves a fundamental disregard for the sequence of historical events. Set in the Civil War period, the novel freely juxtaposes antebellum figures such as Edgar Allan Poe, the Marquis de Sade, General Lafayette and Captain Kidd with references to postwar cultural phenomena such as Buffalo Bill's Wild West Show and Radcliffe College, and figures like T. S. Eliot and Ezra Pound. This disruption serves both to negate the sense of history as a linear evolution, a measure of progress, and to undermine the war's conventional significance as a watershed in African-American history. His basic strategy is an equation between the Civil War itself and the civil unrest of the 1960s, a parallel impressionistically caught in the image of Lincoln's assassination being endlessly replayed in slow motion on the Late News. Upon this foundation he builds an elaborate framework of connections across a century in the situation and experiences of African Americans. Reed's own explanation of this narrative procedure would be in terms of his concept of necromancy: "Necromancers used to lie in the guts of the dead or in tombs to receive visions of the future. That is prophecy. The black writer lies in the guts of old America, making readings about the future."[5] In *Flight to Canada* history is of more analogical than causal significance.

Reed's claim to artistic necromancy is an aspect of the Voodoo aesthetic by which he transforms the slave narrative in *Flight to Canada,* as is the nonlinear model of history in the novel, for Voodoo "teaches that past is present."[6] His aesthetic use of Voodoo also draws upon several other basic characteristics of the religion: it is syncretic, protean, extemporaneous, intuitive and often combative. Reed's appropriation of this last quality is most explicit in *Cab Calloway Stands In for the Moon,* or "D Hexorcism of Noxon D Awful," which he conceived of as a hex upon Nixon;[7] but the sensibility is apparent in the attacks he launches upon diverse detractors and antagonists in all his novels, *Flight to Canada* included. Similarly, Reed's intuitive method is apparent in the analogic method of the novel, its evocation of unstable, often fleeting parallels that are disparately suggestive rather than the components of a logical grid. The Voodoo propensity for improvisation is evident in *Flight to Canada*'s plot development, which is as often generated by the incidental suggestion of a phrase as by the deep structure of the novel. And though the protean qualities of Reed's aesthetic are better seen in earlier novels, *Mumbo Jumbo* in particular, *Flight to Canada* also casually interchanges interior monologue, third- and first-person past and present tense narrative, dream vision, burlesque, elegy and reportage. But the most important quality of Reed's Voodoo aesthetic is its syncretism, because it is at this point that aesthetics and politics meet. He has given it as his main purpose to "humble Judeo-Christian culture," and to affirm instead the plurality of cultures that would characterize more accurately the identity of America.[8] Against the cultural subordination of the "melting pot" he advocates an anti-hierarchical "multiculture." This position originates in his concern to advance African-American culture, a concern which is qualified by his recognition that this culture is suppressed not simply by a dominant rival, but by the principle of monoculturalism it propagates. His polemics and his fiction accordingly include other cultures devalued and denied their place by the dominant tradition in America, embracing Native-American, Oriental, South American and African influences. The syncretism of Voodoo makes it particularly suitable as the aesthetic framework for Reed's multicultural stance: "Voodoo is the perfect metaphor for the multiculture. Voodoo comes out of the fact that all these different tribes and cultures were brought from Africa to Haiti. . . . It's an amalgamation like this country."[9]

The direct source for Reed's aesthetic is actually HooDoo, the African-American version of the Haitian original. The importation of Voodoo into America not only provided it with the African-American pedigree that allows Reed to advance it in the name of both his own culture *and* the principle of multiculturalism; it also involved a process of distillation and accommodation to the existing cultural conditions, which accentuated exactly the qualities Reed values and makes the foundation of his aesthetic. The fusion of an unfamiliar aesthetic with a political position in Reed's "Neo-HooDooism" involved him in extended expositions of the nature and history of HooDoo in his early novels, a process of self-presentation that tended to overshadow the actual use of the aesthetic he was advancing. Certainly his most widely acclaimed novel, *Mumbo Jumbo,* is vulnerable to the charge that it "remains an illustrated HooDoo cookbook" rather than actually being "the dish, a gumbo simmering on the back of a black iron stove."[10] In *Mumbo Jumbo* the dialogue is very often a casual veneer for Reed's own exposition upon the historical pedigree of HooDoo culture: the climactic speech with which PaPa LaBas exposes Hinkle Von Vampton, beginning "it all began 1000s of years ago in Egypt," is the occasion for Reed to

launch into a thirty-page narration of the ancient antipathy of Osiris
and Set and the conspiracy of suppression inflicted upon the followers
of Osiris down through the ages.[11] But *Flight to Canada* suggests a
greater confidence in his aesthetic's capacity to stand by itself, allusions to HooDoo being mainly confined to the novel's first few
pages. Here he affirms the HooDoo inspiration of the poem "Flight
to Canada," the Loa Guede is mentioned, and he refers to the
terminology of possession by a Loa (the host is called a "horse") in
mocking Harriet Beecher Stowe: "*Harriet saying that God wrote* Uncle
Tom's Cabin. *Which God? Some gods will mount any horse.*"[12] These
references are simply pointers and their place is quickly taken by the
polemics of Reed's more particular argument, which concerns not
the history or nature of HooDoo but the equation of multiculturalism
with emancipation, and of America's persisting monoculturalism with
slavery. It is no longer the aesthetic of Neo-HooDooism itself which
is being propagated in the novel's argument, but the political values—
the critique of monoculturalism—by which Reed was impelled to
advance that aesthetic.

By way of Neo-HooDooism, then, Reed is able to return in
Flight to Canada to the slave narrative he had earlier disowned. The
fundamental condition of this return is a transformation of style—he
defies the norms of the genre in almost every aspect of his novel. The
objectives of the slave narrative were primarily to bear witness to the
realities of slavery and to affirm the humanity of the slave against the
brutal conditions that enslaved him. The realization of these priorities
depended upon an accumulation of detail that would give force to
the testimony. Reed, however, proclaims himself a cartoonist. The
slave narrative is constrained by its moral seriousness, while Reed
cultivates irreverent humour: the slave-owner Swille tells Lincoln to
"stop putting your fingers in your lapels like that. You ought to at
least try to polish yourself, man. Go to the theatre. Get some culture"
(28). This disrespect for Lincoln in particular and his nonfictional
characters generally is symptomatic of another of Reed's heresies, his
abuse of historical veracity. His manipulation of these characters is
not an intellectual exploitation of lacunae in the historical record, as
it might be in the hands of E. L. Doctorow, but a flagrantly unhistori-
cal farce. His abuses are always grounded to some degree in an

assumed familiarity with the received text of history, and feed satirically or humorously upon it; their main function is to effect a transformation of the reverent tone handed down in this text by subverting the dignity of its icons.

Implicit in all this is Reed's complete lack of concern with the criteria of realism, upon which the slave narratives depended. His artistic concerns place a lower value on the surface coherence of his narrative than on the imperatives of his fictional argument, or the opportunistic satirical points to which he continually sacrifices narrative continuity. As a result of these priorities, the novel unselfconsciously displays its inconsistencies of character and motivation, illogical narrative developments, loose ends and mismatched plot lines. There is little point in objecting that Reed does not reconcile his perspectives on Lincoln as player and fool, nor provide adequately for the swings in the relationship between Quickskill and the pirate Yankee Jack; that he refers back to Quickskill's dream as an event, and has Yankee Jack and his wife Quaw Quaw united at the opening of the novel, chronologically *after* her discovery that he uses her father's skull as an ashtray. The rationale for these aberrations lies on another plane: Reed refuses to be a slave to his narrative.

Reed's aesthetic decisions are motivated by his concern to affirm the multiculture in the form of his novel, a function for which the form of the original slave narratives is inadequate because of their appropriation as documents for the Abolitionist cause, as Henry Louis Gates has argued: "The political use to which the abolitionists put black literacy demanded a painstaking verisimilitude—a concern with even the most minute concrete detail."[13] As such the slave narratives were denied the freedom of form through which their authors could have expressed *their* culture. And Reed insists that this co-opting of black literature by white liberals is a contemporary problem: "In fact, our worst enemies are radical liberals because they have so much influence on how we look in the media and in American culture. . . . They are only interested in the social realist, the 'experience' of black people. And this treatment limits us and enslaves us."[14]

Reed's revisionary interest in the slave narrative arises from his belief that the forms of slavery still exist in modern America, under the guise of the monoculture's institutionalized subordination of all

other cultures—the institutional structure of slavery remains in sublimated form, as the machinery of a state of oppression he regards as
cultural slavery. The material of the slave narrative therefore allows
Reed to practise his necromancy, exploring the analogies it generates
in the relative positions taken by the various factions of contemporary
culture. But, more than just providing a metaphorical map of the
system of cultural slavery he sees in modern America, he is arguing
for a direct continuity between the two levels, for an evolutionary
transformation of actual into cultural slavery. In doing so, he is also
engaging in the struggle "to get to our aesthetic Canada"[15] by asserting in the novel's form his emancipation from the dictates of the
dominant monoculture.

In *Flight to Canada* the Civil War and the emancipation of the
slaves are equated with the civil rights and black nationalist move-
ments of the 1960s, the social upheaval in both cases leading to an
apparently considerable amelioration of the rights of African Americans. But Reed regards these as limited advances in the progress
towards true emancipation, advances that have succeeded only in
making the mode of oppression more abstract, shifting it from the
material to the cultural realm. He portrays the emancipation of the
slaves as merely a form, devoid of any moral intent—a publicity stunt
by which Lincoln isolates the South in a war over other matters: "We
change the issues, don't you see? Instead of making this some kind of
oratorical minuet about States' Rights versus the Union, what we do
is make it so that you can't be for the South without being for
slavery!" (49). Reed emphasizes the displacement of ethical considerations by political expediency evident in the Emancipation Proclama-
tion, suggesting that neither it nor the reforms of the 1960s indicated
any fundamental transformation in the way in which blacks were
perceived in society, and in fact occurred for essentially pragmatic
reasons. The lack of any revisionary consciousness behind the legisla-
ture ensures that in the cultural sphere, which is largely independent
of the legal framework, blacks experience continuing marginalization.

Reed's caricature of Lincoln is a paradoxical combination of the
idiot yokel of his humble origins and the cunning politician, "Abe
the Player, as history would call him" (13). He first appears seeking
revenue for his war effort by ingratiating himself with the slave-

owner Swille. The description is characteristic of Reed's abbreviated, gestural method, playing against the grain of the archetypal image of innumerable Hollywood and TV Lincolns with a revisionary recasting: "Lincoln, Gary Cooper-awkward, fidgeting with his stovepipe hat, humble-looking, imperfect—a wart here and there—craw and skuttlecoat, shawl, enters the room. 'Mr. Swille, it's a pleasure . . . I'm a small-time lawyer and now I find myself in the room of the mighty . . .' " (22–3). It is later made clear that this is Abe the Player, exploiting his image as a backwoods Hoosier, as he reports to his aide: "First I gave him the yokel-dokel—he saw through that" (45). But it is difficult to distinguish this Lincoln from the one who appears when he abandons the ruse: Reed litters his speech with exclamations like "Well, I'll be dull as a Kansas moon" (47), and has him garble speeches, misunderstand words and confuse his own arguments. Reed heads part two of his novel "Lincoln the Player" not because his Lincoln displays much of the cunning the epithet implies, but because that is the emphasis he wishes to place upon Lincoln's role in the emancipation of the slaves. The morality of the issue is always subordinate to the contingency of practical politics and in fact does not feature at all except where morality itself becomes a political tool. So while the attitude of the "Great Emancipator" towards slavery is hopelessly vague, he builds it into a moral stance on the basis of pure rhetorical appeal: " 'I haven't made my mind up yet, Mr. Swille. I guess I'm a little wishy-washy on the subject still. But . . . well, sometimes I just think that one man enslaving another man is wrong. Is wrong. Is very wrong.' Lincoln pounds the table" (37). It is the demagogic appeal of this role, not its ethical soundness, which ultimately supersedes its political expediency and results in Lincoln's assassination. Swille himself, as the incarnation of the Southern culture Lincoln had affronted, is made responsible for the killing. While condemning Lincoln because he "gave away all that property" (130), Swille does not attribute his downfall to any ideological conflict. He hears with sympathy of Lincoln's affliction with "nigger fever" (131): "Toward the end he kept having visions of himself as a statue. Sitting in the chair and staring out over the Potomac. He started to believe it. He began to see himself as a great Emancipator, Mr. Swille. Got hooked by his own line" (130).

Quickskill's flight from slavery is twice enacted in the book, the first time in his poem "Flight to Canada," which opens the novel; the second time in the narrative that poem generates, both in the sense that it is instrumental in Quickskill's escape to Canada and that it is the germ from which the novel grew (Reed has said that the novel in fact "came out of a poem").[16] The poem's relation to the novel is best understood with reference to Reed's source for the character of his protagonist: "Raven Quickskill, in *Flight to Canada* ... was based more or less on a Tlingit legend—a raven myth."[17] The Raven of the Tlingit Indians is a trickster-creator, capable of mean-spirited pranks, but also of great gifts—he is, as Reed notes, the bringer of light to the tribe (13). It is this opposition which best encapsulates the difference between the Quickskill in the poem and the Quickskill who wrote it. The poem is a vengeful wish fulfilment, a triumphant final confrontation with the hated master that enacts his comprehensive humiliation and, finally, his murder:

> Massa, by the time you gets
> This letter old Sam will have
> Probably took you to the
> Deep Six
>
> That was rat poison I left
> In your Old Crow (5)

The Quickskill in the poem is simply a trickster, using his guile to turn the tables on his master, yet still defined and limited by that relationship, and by his anger. But as the poem's author he is a creator, and asserts his freedom more completely in the demonstration it provides of his cultural autonomy. At this level the violence of his passions is harnessed for his argument, just as Reed's indignation at racial oppression is not allowed to define and limit the subject matter of his writing, but instead is to inform it as a literary act. That creative transcendence permits his argument to do more than a sociological tract: to be itself an assertion and affirmation of his freedom. Quickskill knows that " 'Flight to Canada' was responsible for getting him to Canada. And so for him, freedom was his writing. His writing was his HooDoo" (88–9). Quickskill's means of escape is

cultural; the affirmation of his own aesthetic is a condition of his
material freedom.

While it is as a poet that Quickskill achieves freedom, that is
insufficient in itself. His relationship with Quaw Quaw, the Indian
dancer, presents two attitudes towards the process of emancipation
between which Reed wishes to distinguish. Quaw Quaw wants to
see this evolution in *purely* abstract terms, but Quickskill knows that
his flight to Canada is from the material conditions of slavery, not
from a state of mind. *Material* freedom, *social* equality, is fundamental:
the point is that it is not enough. If the predicament of the African-
American people is translated into individual terms, being liberated
from material slavery but still existing mentally in its thrall is the
condition of the fugitive, a condition in which Quickskill remains as
long as Swille lives. This state is one in which slavery, although no
longer actual, remains the dominant factor in the status the fugitive is
ascribed in the culture. The fugitive is dependent upon the prospect
of abolition, and this dependency results in a new bondage, to the
Abolitionist cause itself. So Quickskill rots in Emancipation City
looking after the houses and cats of his liberal patrons: "That's the
way it was in the fugitive life. Minding things for Abolitionists and
Sympathizers to the Cause" (61). Slavery *is* a state of mind, but in the
same way that being in pain is a state of mind: it reflects real conditions. When Quickskill reaches Canada, he learns that material freedom is not a refuge from racial hatred: "Man, they got a group up
here called the Western Guard, make the Klan look like statesmen"
(160). The attitudes upon which slavery was based still prevail because
although Quickskill has crossed a political border, the culture is
continuous: "as soon as you reach the metropolitan areas you run
into Ford, Sears, Holiday Inn, and all the rest" (160). As the anachronism implies, if the culture is continuous across political frontiers it is
also continuous through time, across such historical frontiers as the
emancipation of the slaves.

Quickskill and Quaw Quaw ultimately differ not on the existence
of a slave mentality but on the means of escaping it. Quaw Quaw is
enamoured of the dominant culture and seeks assimilation, claiming
not to "identify with any group" (165), but Quickskill believes that
assimilation to the monoculture means subordination, marginaliza-

tion. Failing to identify with his own cultural heritage is tantamount to joining forces with the dominant culture to reimpose slavery in sublimated form: "Slaves judged other slaves like the auctioneer and his clients judged them. Was there no end to slavery?" (144).

This betrayal also operates *between* oppressed groups, whose concern for self-advancement engenders a hostility towards each other which mimics that of the establishment and obscures their common oppression. So the fugitive 40s fails to see the irony in his nationalistic loathing of immigrants: "The Nativists got good ideas. So do the Know-Nothings. I'd join them if they let me" (77). Quickskill is himself guilty of this destructive competitiveness between minorities when he involves himself in a parodic shouting match with the Jewish immigrant Mel Leer, each adamant that his people have suffered the most. Their argument is the product of competition for liberal establishment patronage, the prospect of which breeds hostility between potential allies. Reed's long-running confrontation with black feminists principally concerns this issue, Reed charging that they have peddled a stereotypical reactionary view of the black male to the white literary establishment, betraying their race in the interests of their feminism. The argument is carried forward in *Flight to Canada* in the rival interests of the slaves and the suffragettes. Quickskill is himself betrayed when his poem is brought to the notice of Swille via an outraged feminist who objects that "In the poem he refers to our women in a most anti-suffragette manner" (51). Reed values cultural liberation above women's liberation, and ridicules the reversal of this priority in the character of the slave-owner's wife, Ms. Swille. She goes on a hunger strike, protesting that having to feed herself is anti-suffragette. At the same time she claims sisterhood with her house slaves: "Today she called me and Bangalang her sisters and said something about all of us being in the same predicament. Me and Bangalang just looked at each other" (59). But the issue is not confined to the explicit political argument of the novel, because it evidently has roots in Reed's basic assumptions about gender roles. The relationship between Quaw Quaw and Quickskill suggests that a degree of sexual machismo is involved in his position, and the form of their relationship (despite his insistence upon their age difference) is also essentially paternalistic.

Nonetheless, Reed's concern is above all for solidarity, which in the relationship between Quickskill and Quaw Quaw means solidarity both between the sexes and between African and Native Americans. The scene in which they make love is punctuated by excerpts from *Our American Cousin* (the production attended by Lincoln is being televised): the occasion, in other words, is that on which the continuity of their oppression is confirmed by Lincoln's assassination. Reed takes excerpts from the play which are abusive to Indians and blacks and alternates them with descriptions of sex in which he sometimes appears careful to avoid any hint of domination: "They started to move in a seesaw fashion. Then there was some hip-swiveling and bending backwards" (101). The novel hardly does enough to silence Reed's feminist critics, but it does attribute qualities to Quaw Quaw that lend some weight to his claim that "women in general make out better in my books than black men do in the works of black women and white women, feminist writers."[18]

The question of the cultural element of slavery and the problem of the true nature of the road to emancipation are united in the novel by the figure of Harriet Beecher Stowe. Her implied presence in *Flight to Canada*—the whole of Part One is titled "Naughty Harriet," and copies of *Uncle Tom's Cabin* make repeated incidental appearances—far exceeds the actual direct attention paid her in the text, which is confined to a few pages at the beginning and end of the novel. But her structurally enhanced role is justified by the dual thematic significance Reed places upon her: she is herself made to represent cultural slavery by Reed's account of her source for *Uncle Tom's Cabin*; and his examination of the modes of revolt against slavery is conducted in terms of the pejorative meaning of "Uncle Tom" in contemporary usage.

Reed freely acknowledges that his charge of plagiarism against Stowe is a tongue-in-cheek abuse of the scant evidence behind Josiah Henson's later reputation as the original Uncle Tom: "I was having fun with Harriet Beecher Stowe, saying that she took her plot in *Uncle Tom's Cabin* from Josiah Henson. You know, they did meet when she was four. . . ."[19] But the fiction provides Reed with a paradigm for his concept of cultural slavery. Against *Uncle Tom's Cabin* he sets Henson's own autobiography:

The Life of Josiah Henson, Formerly a Slave. Seventy-seven pages
long. It was short, but it was his. It was all he had. His story. A
man's story is his gris-gris, you know. Taking his story is like
taking his gris-gris. The thing that is himself. It's like robbing a
man of his Etheric Double. People pine away. (8)

This plagiarism therefore stands for the cultural appropriation by
which minority cultures are suppressed, and for the consequent oppression of their people, the essence of Reed's metaphor of slavery.
Set alongside Henson's obscurity, the enormous success of *Uncle
Tom's Cabin* becomes a sinister allegory of the perpetuation of slavery
in cultural terms—a slavery which is no longer confined to the
South: "Harriet made enough money on someone else's plot to buy
thousands of silk dresses and a beautiful home, 'one of those spacious
frame mansions of bland and hospitable mien which the New England joiners knew so well how to build.' A Virginia plantation in
New England" (9). Henry Louis Gates rightly sees the issue involved
here as political, the control of history being at stake: "Reed is
writing about what Robert Burns Stepto has called 'narrative control'—the possession of one's own story, be that our collective history
or even one's very own autobiography."[20] But of more particular
concern to Reed is the cultural oppression, the exclusion not just of
Josiah Henson from his story, but also of his way of telling it.

   Reed distinguishes between the cultural aspect of emancipation
and the long-established equation of a slave's freedom with his or
her education. He cites Frederick Douglass, whose autobiography
emphatically links literacy with freedom, as a precedent for his own
protagonist, who "was the first one of Swille's slaves to read, the first
to write and the first to run away" (14). But the novel also presents a
literate slave, Cato, who remains absolutely servile. His self-
immolation before the monoculture is characterized not only by his
repudiation of the sentiments of "Flight to Canada," but also by his
disavowal of its style. In the attack upon Quickskill's poem by which
he aligns himself aesthetically with his oppressors he unintentionally
burlesques the vocabulary of the literary review: "And if you ask me,
it don't have no redeeming qualities, it is bereft of any sort of *pièce de
résistance,* is cute and unexpurgated . . ." (52). Cato is a debased ver-

sion of Quaw Quaw; while she believes her own art has a place
within the monoculture, he simply renounces his culture. He regards
ingratiating himself with the slave-owners, through the flattery of
imitation, as his best chance for self-improvement. But the inevitable
transparency of this imitation makes it simply a confirmation of the
cultural inferiority to which he has consented: by accepting his masters' evaluation of his culture, he sanctions his own oppression.

While Cato seeks assimilation into the monoculture, Quickskill
has to actively fight it. He meets William Wells Brown on the way
to Canada, and informs him of the literary discipleship that influenced
"Flight to Canada," while predicting that the white establishment
will suppress any such suggestion of an independent cultural tradition.
The language of literary influence here makes explicit the connection
between cultural and actual slavery: "It kind of imitates your style,
though I'm sure the critics are going to give me some kind of white
master" (121). The cultural appropriation Quickskill fears is not a
token of acceptance but the mechanism of oppression itself. In *Mumbo
Jumbo* it is one of the principal methods for the suppression of "Jes
Grew" advocated by Hinkle Von Vampton: "we will feature the
Talking Android who will tell the J.G.C.s that Jes Grew is not ready
and owes a large debt to Irish Theatre. This Talking Android will
Wipe That Grin Off Its Face. He will tell it that it is derivative."[21]

The monoculture is signified in *Flight to Canada* by the culture of
the antebellum South, the incarnation of which is Quickskill's master,
Swille. The power of this culture is evidenced by Swille's complete
autonomy: he stands aloof from the Civil War and condescends to
both Lincoln and Davis. The monoculture is sustained by slavery, a
denial of the humanity of a people which is itself made possible in
Reed's scenario by monocultural dogma: the denial of the slaves'
cultural validity is central to the rationale by which they are oppressed. Quickskill's poetry, he is told by the Nebraska tracers who
come to repossess him, is collected in *"The Anthology of Ten Slaves,*
they had it in the anthropology section of the library" (63). The same
process of cultural disqualification is encapsulated in the suppression
of non-Christian religious practices, of the African gods of HooDoo,
providing a mirror for the relation of Reed's Neo-HooDoo aesthetic
to the contemporary literary mainstream. It is the principle that

reduces the slaves' capacity for rebellion to a physiological disorder, a mechanical fault: Reed notes the contributions to medical science of Dr. Samuel Cartwright, who diagnosed rogue slaves as suffering from "*Dysaesthesia Aethipica,*" and runaways as the victims of "*Drapeto-mania*" (18). The desire for autonomy is alien to the constitution of a slave, whose faculties are restricted to those required by the slave-master. This constriction of the slave's cultural and personal identity leads eventually to the legal position Southern culture required—a slave is property, a material thing. Reed satirizes this denial of identity through Swille's attempt at a reasoned response to his runaways, which involves regarding them simultaneously as objects and, for the purpose of moral condemnation, as persons: "Look, Robin, if they'd came to me and if they'd asked to buy themselves, perhaps we could have arranged terms. But they didn't; they furtively pilfered themselves" (19).

Uncle Robin, Quickskill's counterpart, approaches emancipation by a different route, but it is Reed's assertion that the principle of *cultural* dissent remains the same. Uncle Robin parallels Harriet Beecher Stowe's Uncle Tom in name and situation, and Reed makes the analogy quite explicit by representing him as a rejected alternative protagonist for her novel: the servile house slave Cato goads him, "She didn't even use your interview. Used Tom over at the Legree plantation" (55). Uncle Robin is the focus of Reed's enquiry into the forms of Uncle Tomism in the current sense, one who is submissively loyal or servile to whites, a self-interested capitulator to the value system of the oppressor. Reed provides several instances of Uncle Robin tommying to Swille as his position demands, but there is always an undertone of irony which qualifies his behaviour. He extols the comforts of life on the Swille plantation: "We gets whipped with a velvet whip, and there's free dental care and always a fiddler case your feet get restless" (37). There is a similar irony in his dealings with the true Uncle Toms of Swille's household, Cato and Moe, both of whom he aids in their attempts to ingratiate themselves with Swille by providing some spot remover for stains on their clothing; the context of these incidents clearly suggests a metaphorical play upon "skin whitener." And despite his piety in Swille's presence, Uncle Robin does not share the Christian devotion of Stowe's character. When Judy quotes the Bible, "He that knoweth his master's will and doeth it not, shall be beaten with many stripes," he responds, "I never read it, but I figured something like that was in it" (57). He is not an Uncle Tom, but an unreconciled slave with a long-term strategy. He has not accepted his servitude any more than the three runaways, Quickskill, 40s and Leechfield; and in fact these three all come to display elements of Uncle Tomism themselves. 40s and Leechfield represent two further types of rebellion, 40s the paramilitary and Leechfield the black marketeer. But 40s runs away only to perpetuate his own oppression by failing to escape the mentality of the fugitive, existing in an outlaw state of armed readiness. His reliance on violent means provides his oppressors with a stereotype of barbarism and abandons the assertion of his full humanity. He has put himself beyond the pale of cultural emancipation, of the power of words upon which Quickskill relies: "you take the words; give me the rifle. That's the only word I need. R-i-f-l-e. Click" (81).

Leechfield's entrepreneurial ability is starved outside the black market context of slavery in which it thrived. He cannot legitimize his talent, and therefore reinvents that context. He turns to selling himself, the only "property" left available to him, and his talent becomes a facet of his disenfranchisement: " 'I'll Be Your Slave for One Day.' Leechfield was standing erect. In small type underneath the picture it said 'Humiliate Me. Scorn Me' " (80). He attempts to purchase his freedom, accepting his status as merchandise, and aspiring only to control of the profits: "I sent the money to Swille. I bought myself with the money with which I sell myself. If anybody is going to buy and sell me, it's going to be me" (73).

But Quickskill, only able to operate in the shadow of slavery by minding houses for abolitionists and doing antislavery lectures, is also effectively selling himself. Like Leechfield, he has been deluded by a materialistic equation between money and freedom: Leechfield seeks to buy himself from Swille; Quickskill, to pay his passage to Canada. But Swille does not accept Leechfield's payment, and the material Canada cannot fulfil Quickskill's expectations. Neither finds it possible to climb out of slavery on the back of material success, because slavery is not a wholly material condition. Uncle Robin, in his rebuke to Leechfield, provides the argument for the spiritual element in social emancipation: "Did you really think that it was just a matter of economics? . . . He didn't want money. He wanted the slave in you. . . . That was the conflict between you and Swille. You, 40s and Quickskill threatened to give the god in the slave breath" (177).

Uncle Tomism, Reed is suggesting, has many guises, and often the forms of collaboration with the oppressor are confused with the forms of revolt. By depending on violence, 40s concedes the law to the white establishment; by depending on economics, Leechfield and to some extent Quickskill locate their emancipation at the material level, and acquiesce in a higher, cultural subservience. By compromising and making ambiguous the modes of escaping oppression, Reed subverts the modern consensus that "You have to be angry. There's only one mask that you can wear."[22] In fact it is Uncle Robin's guise which prevails most effectively. Swille dies according to the conventions of a Poesque gothic tale, the decadent culture collapsing from the violence of its own internal contradictions. But the end was near anyway, as Uncle Robin had substituted Coffee Mate (Reed gives a list of ingredients) for the two gallons of slave mothers' milk Swille consumed each morning. Having consulted his gods, Uncle Robin decides to "work Taneyism right back on him" (171), and falsifies the will.[23] On his newly inherited Virginia plantation, Uncle Robin muses upon the nature of freedom and how to attain it: "Yeah, they get down on me an Tom. But who's the fool? Nat Turner or us? Nat said he was going to do this. Was going to do that. . . . Now Nat's dead and gone for these many years, and here I am, master of a dead man's house" (178). Reed sets the vilified Uncle Tom against the more heroic model of Nat Turner, as paradigms of the slave inside and outside the system. With a little twist, Uncle Tom comes out on top. Robin knows, as Quickskill discovers, that Canada is simply an idea of freedom. Stepping outside of reality in pursuit of an idea is not the way to change that reality; but working on the inside, Robin is able to reach a position from which he can "take this fifty rooms of junk and make something useful out of it" (179). Accordingly, the narrative ends not in Canada, but with Quickskill's return to Virginia. That is the rationale of Reed's revisionary slave narrative: his aesthetic breaks the shackles of the monoculture, but he does not run away.

Reed's position, like Baraka's, constitutes a move beyond the separatist politics of black nationalism: both perceived that nationalism could only be a stage in the struggle of African Americans, and that this struggle was part of a larger conflict. But their responses diverged at that point—while Baraka seized upon class and advocated revolutionary socialism, Reed engaged in a series of editorial and publishing enterprises aimed at the affirmation of a multicultural society.[24] These publishing ventures as much as anything stigmatize Reed as a capitulationist in Baraka's eyes, but in terms of Reed's argument the positions are virtually reversed. Baraka subordinates cultural equality to the realization of a postrevolutionary economic equality: in the interim, black literature should be the servant of the revolution. But for Reed such an aesthetic preserves an outlaw separatist agenda entirely amenable to the hierarchies of the white literary establishment. Because for him culture is not merely superstructure, but the primary repository of a minority group's identity, such an aesthetic effectively capitulates to a state of oppression. Reed's demonstrations of American cultural diversity, on the other hand, confront the monoculture with its own partiality and compel a revolution in America's concept of itself.

Chapter 4

Narrative Inscription, History and the Reader in Robert Coover's *The Public Burning*

Robert Coover's early novels established his interest in the ways our various explanatory narratives impose upon the truth of our experience. His exploration of these ideas was at its most abstract in the stories of *Pricksongs and Descants* (1969), but it gained a political edge in *The Public Burning,* where he addressed the Rosenberg executions and the climate of McCarthyism from which they resulted. The novel displayed a new emphasis upon the specifics of recent American history in Coover's work, to the extent that he was obliged to conduct a large part of the final editing under considerable pressure from the house lawyers at Viking.[1] It both recreated and transformed the ideological narratives of 1950s' Cold War orthodoxy in order to explore the ways in which they inscribed both populace and protagonists, compelling them towards a deadly resolution. At the same time the argument itself worked towards an equivalent affective inscribing of the reader, raising questions about the necessary conditions for moral judgement.

Fundamental to Coover's strategy in *The Public Burning* is a surprisingly unsympathetic treatment of the Rosenbergs themselves. They are kept at a cool distance throughout, even though the chapters narrated by Nixon are largely devoted to his (self-interested) attempts at reaching an understanding of them. Nixon's intensive study does not approach an imaginative empathy with the Rosenbergs but appropriates their story to his own life. He pursues relentlessly the parallels between the upbringing, experiences and character of Julius Rosenberg and his own, construing their lives as mirror images of each other and thus, in the process of assessing where Julius deviated from the Horatio Alger career profile, establishing his own adherence to that narrative. His analysis of Julius remains always subordinate to his obsessive self-analysis, maintaining the priority of the political aspirations which underlie his interest in the Rosenbergs. The one apparent exception to this surprising exclusion of the Rosenbergs themselves from a story to which they are so central is the chapter in which Nixon and Ethel Rosenberg meet at Sing Sing. But the Ethel presented here is wholly mysterious—the narrative by this point is so far implicated in Nixon's own psychological journey that she is scarcely allowed any reality independent of him, becoming merely a foil to his fantasies. This is intimated in the transformation that occurs in her when they meet, Nixon's first unfavourable comparison of her appearance to his fantasy image being superseded as she approaches by her metamorphosis into just this image. She plays out her role entirely according to his preconceptions, moving from cold rhetoric to hidden weakness to unbridled passion. And even though she goes on to exceed and betray his fantasy with the lipsticked message "I AM A SCAMP" that she scrawls across his buttocks, this too derives from Nixon's own imagination, his masochistic fascination with Ethel's past treatment of strike breakers: "When a delivery truck tried to crash the picket line, Ethel and the girls hauled the driver from his cab, stripped him bare, and lipsticked his butt with I AM A SCAB. My own butt tingled with the thought of it" (304). The whole scene, in other words, is generated out of Nixon's psychology and serves to lay it bare. The narrative attention is focussed so single-mindedly upon this objective that no room is left for any insight into Ethel Rosenberg at all. Like Nixon's analysis of the Rosenbergs' past, it has meaning only in relation to him, and reveals nothing about her to which the reader can adhere.

Beyond this, the Rosenbergs' direct presence in the novel is limited to the quotations from their Death House letters and from Ethel's clemency appeals. These too are for the most part given in support of Nixon's theory that the Rosenbergs are consumed by the roles in which they have cast themselves, and so they operate exactly against the intimacy direct quotation would otherwise offer. Nor is Nixon's theory so unreasonable as to be purely a projection of his own

obsessions (though it is that as well). Coover needs it to explain the
Rosenbergs' strange behaviour at the trial, and later in prison, where
the Warden reports them "behaving in what they probably think of
as, well, symbolic ways—you know, acting like they're establishing
historical models or precedents or something."[2] It is also an explanation to which Coover himself alluded when he criticized Louis
Nizer's *The Implosion Conspiracy* for "accepting the Rosenbergs'
courtroom role-playing at face value," and asked, "was the cause for
their suspicious courtroom behaviour in fact their pretending to be
somebody they were not during the trial?"[3] In the third of the novel's
"intermezzos," in which the tone is usually at its most direct, Julius
and Ethel's letters are used to create an extended statement of their
stand against the pressures upon them to confess, under a title calculated to give maximum force to its melodramatic content—"Human
Dignity is Not for Sale: A Last-Act Sing Sing Opera" (381). In spite
of the use to which it is put this is not a pejorative representation of
the Rosenbergs, as is made clear at the beginning of the second
intermezzo, a dramatization of Ethel's clemency appeal to Eisenhower, in which her histrionic rhetoric is rationalized: "At no time
during the dialogue does the PRESIDENT address the PRISONER,
or even acknowledge her presence on the same stage. The PRIS-
ONER, aware of this, sometimes speaks to him directly, but more
often seems to be trying to reach him by bouncing echoes off the
Audience" (247). In their hopeless situation, the suggestion that the
Rosenbergs have adopted strategic roles carries no satiric charge, as it
does in the case of Nixon himself. It does ensure that even the limited
presence they do have in the narrative is discredited, and invalidated
as a focus of reader identification. Clearly Coover is not concerned
with a novelistic identification with the Rosenbergs, and therefore
forfeits the sort of empathetic recreation of their martyrdom that
would have generated the greatest emotional force from the story.
But the cost of such an approach would have been to alienate the
reader from the prevailing mentality of fifties' America, the entire
atmosphere of Cold War hysteria that condemned them. It is this
phenomenon with which Coover is most concerned, and in which
he seeks partially to implicate the reader.
     This does not involve him in a vitriolic attack upon the Rosen-

bergs, because while full identification with them would tend to make the neuroses of Cold War America inaccessible, a vague humanistic sympathy fails even to raise the question, is easily compatible with these same neuroses and readily assimilated to the very ideology responsible for their deaths. Even Nixon is able to take a stand on this issue: "On the other hand, let me say—and I don't mind being controversial on this subject—I was a little sorry that two people, a father and mother of two little boys, had to die" (84). This mention of the children exposes the point at which rigorously separated ideological and emotional impulses meet in the novel: the American people, while deploring (with Eisenhower their spokesman) the way in which the children are used by Ethel in her clemency appeals, nevertheless consume the pathos of their situation avidly. The process is described in the Times Square revels, where entertainers compete in dramatizing the Rosenbergs' Death House letters as the hour of execution approaches: "Jimmy Durante and Gary Moore come out and play it for pathos, using the letters to the children. Out front the people glance up at the Paramount clock, their eyes filling with tears of laughter and unabashed sentiment . . ." (428). Coover's strategy is to frame this camping of pathos in his novel with the spectacle of its consumption. A story in The New York Times the day after the executions reported the eldest child accidentally hearing that his parents' final appeal had been denied in a newsflash during the baseball game he was watching.[4] It is a moving piece, but rigorously avoids any transition from the emotional to the political level. Coover uses the pathos of the incident, but at the same time makes the reader's consumption of it self-conscious by dwelling upon the function of media in the incident: both the boy's experience of the casual transition the television offers him, from baseball to the imminent death of his parents and back to baseball, and his awareness that his response is also being observed (by the readership of The New York Times). He pronounces his lines as reported in the Times, "feeling that someone or something is watching him" (277) but yet that "Nobody's listening" (278).

Conversely, at the Times Square executions Cecil B. De Mille augments the event with a documentary on the children projected against the Claridge Hotel—"Americans, as he knows, go ape over sentiment" (511)—but within this satiric frame Coover himself uses images from the film to heighten his own description of the electrocution scene. This description is actually a powerful combination of three distinct narrative techniques. There is the appeal to elemental but already compromised emotional reactions through interpolated scenes from the documentary and carefully selected, touching but apolitical extracts from the Rosenbergs' letters. There is the impersonal narrative voice which speaks, as throughout the novel, from within the ideology it describes, its emphasis upon the scene's qualities as spectacle become the principal vehicle of a satiric argument here reaching its most brutal level: "There are some out in the audience who have been feeling they've seen all there is to see the first time around—you just plug them in, they twitch and jerk awhile and shit their pants, then you unplug them and cart them off, ho hum . . . but Ethel's entrance has changed all that" (512–13). But there is also a descriptive mode that works against both the intrusive double movement of this ironic voice and the comforting sentimentality to which the more directly emotive passages appeal. This derives its force from the dispassionately minute specificity by which it proceeds, recording as neutrally as possible every nightmarish detail of the electrocution process. It is a narrative technique that responds to Nixon's critique of the Rosenberg letters, which isolates the point at which they cease to convince: "But then came the death sentence, and what was striking about all their letters after that was the almost total absence in them of concrete reality, of real-life involvement—it was all hyperbole, indignation, political cliché, abstraction" (305). He goes on to contrast his own effective use of specific detail in his "Checkers" speech: "Where they had lathered their Death House letters with sententious generalities . . . I had named names and places and times" (310). Nixon's understanding of political rhetoric triumphs over the Rosenbergs': Coover's clinical descriptions in the execution scene redress the balance. But the ruthless detail by which he charts their deaths is not Coover's plea for the Rosenbergs, only a clear-eyed realization of the facts of execution. The fate of the Rosenbergs as individuals is not central to the novel's argument. This circumstance has caused a certain amount of critical distress: Richard Andersen's analysis of the novel, for example, suffers from his assumption that it is attempting an engaging rendition of the Rosenbergs and failing in that attempt. The result of this misguided approach is apparent in such assessments as "Though often moving, their words lack introspection and occasionally seem rhetorical," which rather understates the case in its efforts at moderate judgement.[5] If the Rosenbergs themselves do not ultimately concern Coover neither does the degree of their innocence or guilt, though he has expressed a firm opinion on the issue elsewhere: "If you read the trial record ... you pretty much have to conclude that the Rosenbergs were innocent of the charges against them. But they were either responsible for protecting some other secret, or believed themselves to be."[6] But in the novel this interpretation of the reality behind the public record is put into the mouth of Richard Nixon, and *he,* at the novel's climax, is there at the head of the crowd rushing to pull the switch on Ethel. The actual innocence or guilt of the Rosenbergs was a minor issue among the forces that took them to their deaths: the title of his novel indicates that Coover places the emphasis upon the American public themselves. His concern is with the collective mind of America at the time of the executions: the ways in which its attitudes and responses conform to perceptions of the political situation modelled upon religious and mythical narratives, and acted out in ritualistic manner by the entire nation.

The fundamental manipulation by which Coover transforms his narrative from a historical fiction into a metaphorical realization of the fiction behind history is the transposition (offered deadpan in the first paragraph of the prologue) of the Rosenbergs' executions from the death chamber at Sing Sing to a stage in the middle of Times Square: "their fate ... is at last sealed, and it is determined to burn them in New York City's Times Square on the night of their fourteenth wedding anniversary, Thursday, June 18, 1953" (3). The matter-of-fact tone, achieved by displacing the emphasis onto the wedding anniversary and slipping in his divergence from history incidentally in midsentence, establishes it as no more nor less extraordinary than the historical information that surrounds it. This fusion of literal and metaphorical creates a narrative space that is both and neither, where analytic metaphor and historical fact can operate together without the mediation of an authorial narrator. Coover has said in interview that "Stories tend to appear to me, not as formal ideas, but as metaphors, and these metaphors seem to demand structures of their own."[7] This structure is apparent in *The Public Burning*, the founding metaphor that suggests itself being contained in the simple proposition that the Rosenbergs were scapegoats.

By developing this metaphor, Coover is able to tease out all the overtones of primitive ritual in the scapegoat role the Rosenbergs fulfilled in the McCarthy Era, and create a full blown sacrificial rite in which the whole tribe of America participates. The metaphor owes an acknowledged debt to Arthur Miller's *The Crucible,* which Coover has playing on execution night to an audience of one, the author. "Ah well: art . . ." he broods, "not as lethal as one might hope . . ." (490). Coover's own art, at over twenty years distance, is offered more as analysis than as polemic. He takes quite literally the Manicheanism of the Cold War rhetoric that dominated the period, translating it into the scripture of a sect whose forces of Light, under the aegis of Uncle Sam, are besieged by the communist Phantom's forces of Darkness. That such a translation is so simply effected gives an authority to the metaphor that compels attention throughout the considerable length and intricacy to which he extends it—and he is able to turn an enormous quantity of the public record of the time to his purpose. The first intermezzo, "The War Between the Sons of Light and the Sons of Darkness," is subtitled "The Vision of Dwight David Eisenhower (from Public Papers of the Presidents, January 20–June 19, 1953)" (149); and in this collage of quotations Coover is able to establish an extraordinary insistence upon the metaphors of light and darkness and the religion of the American Way. "It was as though he'd never really believed in God," observes Nixon, "until he discovered Him there in the Declaration of Independence" (184).

The susceptibility to Coover's analysis of the behaviour and events surrounding the Rosenberg executions suggests a link far more tangible than the trick of a metaphor; it suggests that the rhetoric and thought of Cold War America tapped into the substantial and insidious power of religious thought, superstition and ultimately the anthropological propensities of the American people. Coover's anthropological interest is apparent in his characterization of the Times Square chapters in terms of a concept he borrows from Roger Caillois: " 'Dreamtime' is a ritual return to the mythic roots of a group of people. . . . This idea of a ritual bath of prehistoric or preconscious experience was very attractive to me as I began developing the Rosenberg book."[8] The Manichean cult he imposes upon the climate of fifties' America is therefore of interpretative value not just in itself but as an example of the way the politics of a modern society may draw strength from unacknowledged primitive models. The gathering in Times Square is an instance of the "collective effervescence" by which Durkheim characterized all religious or quasi-religious assembly. But while Durkheim held the creative power of such occasions in high regard, Coover's view is much less optimistic. The function of the Rosenberg executions is presented as reaching beyond the fulfilment of doctrinal expectations to the satisfaction of more fundamental needs. On the morning of the executions all America wakes in a state of sexual excitement: "But none, curiously enough, has used his or her aroused sexuality on a mate, it's as though, somehow, that's not what it was all about . . ." (164). The electrocutions are sanctioned by the harmony between their political motivations and the deep psychological needs of the American public.

The displaced source of these needs is revealed by the episode in which a moviegoer, after seeing the 3-D movie, *House of Wax,* walks out onto the street without removing his cardboard glasses. The surreal and slapstick scenes that result serve as his own private descent into "dreamtime," exposing his deepest fears: "It's all coming together . . . into the one image that has been pursuing him through all his sleepless nights, the billowing succubus he's been nurturing for nine months now, ever since the new hydrogen-bomb tests at Eniwetok: yes, the final spectacle, the one and only atomic holocaust, he's given birth to it at last" (286). In a standard carnivalesque inversion, the crazy distortions of the 3-D glasses are fundamentally truthful, expressing the madness of the country's psychological state. As beneficiary of these insights, the man himself "is very clear-headed, which is the main cause of his panic. It strikes him that he is perhaps the only sane man left on the face of the earth" (287). He remains, however, a representative American, and the irreconcilable opposition between his personal insight and the public creed required of him leads him to throw himself into the chair on the Times

Square set, his words serving as a satiric literalization of Eisenhower's rhetoric: "*The President said it: 'the one capital offense is a lack of staunch faith!' THROW THE SWITCH!*" (288). The lengths to which Coover pursues his metaphor are grotesque, but it is the force of insight behind it that allows him to extend and elaborate it so fully, and continue to surprise with new points of contact between trope and history.

Summoned into being by this metaphor is the figure of Uncle Sam, who is deity and high priest to the sect, both the product of the unfolding American narrative and its orchestrator. This religious authority is grounded in his identification with the American folk consciousness: he is an amalgam of every popular hero from Davie Crockett to Superman, possessed of a rich folk vernacular which draws its imagery and rhetoric from the frontier experience and is given free rein throughout the novel. He is a character burdened with the history of a nation but who eludes the ironies this generates by appealing to exactly the complexities of motivation and personality created by the equation between nation and character. So, dismissing his flagrant contempt for the Constitution in the Rosenberg case, he scoffs: "Bah! The wild oats of youth! . . . puritanism! whoo, worse'n acne! It's great for stirrin' up the jism when you're nation-breedin', but it ain't no way to live a life!" (531). The expediency of character takes precedence over any commitment to the historical imperatives of a national constitution. The novel's evocation of American folk consciousness has been examined at length by David Estes, who notes that its barbaric values are preserved through an engaging humour.[9] As Estes presents it, this is pure diagnosis on Coover's part; but his use of folk humour in the novel also makes a sly appeal to the reader. In the case of Uncle Sam, it generates a degree of affection quite at odds with the ethical response he provokes, and disconcerted critics have objected that he is simply not dislikable enough, finding it "hard to remember that he represents anything worse than the national talent for garrulousness."[10]

Uncle Sam's role in the novel is complicated by functions other than that of personified national character. He is also the spiritual force that animates the president, his incarnation, and as such he is part accumulated heritage of the presidency—his looks are an eclectic

sum of the features of past presidents—and part abstraction of the
electorate, the spirit of enfranchised American opinion. This representative function is most apparent in his encounter with maverick
Justice William Douglas, to whom the book is dedicated. Having
granted the Rosenbergs a stay of execution, Douglas is confronted by
Uncle Sam in the Supreme Court. Douglas is the only character in
the novel who stands up to Uncle Sam, but his defence of the stay of
execution here serves only to whip the nation's embodiment into a
blustering fury (later it earns Douglas a public spanking, though
Coover's sympathies demand that he remain cool and sardonic
through even this ordeal). As he walks out of the Supreme Court
chamber he meets the janitor, who sees only an empty room: " 'You
talkin' to yo'self?' 'Yeah,' says Douglas without turning back. 'It
looks that way . . . ' " (78). All these elements in Uncle Sam have a
role in furthering the inexorable movement towards the executions
of which he is the architect. Personifying them in a character allows
Coover to consider them in a way which is both intimate and
analytical. As a character Uncle Sam, for all the vice Coover displays
in him, evokes a response complex enough to challenge the reader
with complicity in the ideology he represents. He holds a fascination
which inhabits his worst excesses, and as such forbids the easy condemnation his (or America's) behaviour would otherwise invite. The
creation of Uncle Sam also crucially involves giving the national
character a consciousness of its own, enabling him to articulate and
act upon the implicit desires and fears of a generation. In this way
matter that would be restricted to discursive interpretation and diagnosis in a less radical novelistic approach becomes a forceful, persistent
presence and prime mover in the novel. Recognizing the value of
character but addressing abstract issues, Coover has turned the latter
into the former, and so enabled his presentation of what would
otherwise have been a thematically overburdened argument.

Uncle Sam's role, especially in presiding over the Times Square
ritual sacrifice, is that of ringmaster; part of Coover's larger structural
concept of *The Public Burning* as a three-ring circus. According to this
framework, the different types of chapters (impersonally narrated,
Nixon narrated and intermezzos) correspond to the three rings, and
Nixon plays the clown to Uncle Sam's ringmaster. This structural

concept combines two elements, carnival and performance, which are intimately related to the substance of the novel. Coover's use of the carnivalesque, according to the specification provided by Mikhail Bakhtin, is apparent throughout. The Nixon chapters harp ceaselessly upon the Rabelaisian motifs of Bakhtin's "material bodily principle"—Nixon's grotesque appetites, his sexuality, his smell, his increasingly shabby appearance, masturbation, flatulence, urination, defecation, buggery and his public exposure on the Times Square stage. In the impersonal chapters carnivalesque action builds in a crescendo as events in Times Square progress: an example is the slapstick scene in which the Supreme Court Justices who have earlier vacated a stay of execution flounder ignominiously in a pile of GOP elephant droppings. A rigorous penal code is in operation here—not just the simple inversion of rank that characterises carnivalesque in general but a much more specific degradation according to merit regarding the Rosenberg case. So Justices Douglas and Black, who opposed the overruling, escape the ordeal—as does Justice Frankfurter, who hovers on the brink but is spared for his belated choice of the dissenting camp. A similar principle works in the stampede for the electrocution switch at the novel's climax, where it is darkly intimated that pre-eminence in this race is a gauge for the participant's future role in American history: "they all rush forward . . . scrambling up over the side of the stage, fighting for position as though their very future depended on it, racing for the switch—it's hard to tell who gets his hands on it first, maybe the Vice-President with his head start . . . or young Senator Kennedy, more athletic than most . . ." (517).

The distinction has to be drawn, though, between carnivalesque in the narrative and the subject matter as carnival, for the latter, despite appearances, is significantly not the case. The structure of the novel as circus implies the subjugation of carnival through presentation or performance, the use of controlled carnival for tendentious purposes by ringmaster Uncle Sam. The function of the gathering in Times Square is to satisfy the primitive demands of the people with a simulation of carnival disorder—a logical extension of the scapegoat function fulfilled by the Rosenbergs. Or, in Durkheim's terms, it is a gathering of the tribe in order to consolidate their faith by participating in the effervescence of religious assembly: "This is why all parties, political, economic or confessional, are careful to have periodical reunions where their members may revivify their common faith by manifesting it in common."[11] "Oh, I don't reckon we could live like this all year round," says Uncle Sam, "But we do need us an occasional peak of disorder and danger to keep things from just peterin' out, don't we?" (95). The carefully contrived framework within which the festivities are allowed to take place betrays the hand of a manipulative Uncle Sam, as the embodiment of the national interest aloof from the people who should define it. As such, carnival is used as a generator of orthodoxy: the only genuine occurrences of carnivalesque in the narrative are in fact disruptive of this doctrinaire show, not allied to it. The detail of Bakhtin's concept of carnival makes clear discrimination possible. Carnival, for him, is spontaneous, and not to be equated with politically organized festivals: the Times Square burnings are minutely organized by Uncle Sam and his deputies. Carnival, as distinct from official occasions, involves the suspension of hierarchical rank, norms and prohibitions, but rank is rigorously observed in Times Square through the provision of a VIP enclosure and the parade of dignitaries before the crowd; and the whole purpose of the occasion is the consolidation of anticommunist norms and the punishment of transgression. Bakhtin's carnival is the instrument of truth, exposing the formal impositions of dominant narratives—rather than reinforcing them, as is the function of the Rosenberg executions for the dualistic framework of Uncle Sam and the Phantom.

Coover's narrative itself, however, does possess all these properties, and another lacking in the Times Square festival which goes to the centre of his use of the carnivalesque. This is the particular function of carnival laughter, which Bakhtin distinguishes from straight satire: "Carnival laughter . . . is directed at all and everyone, including the carnival's participants. . . . This is one of the essential differences of the people's festive laughter from the pure satire of modern times. The satirist whose laughter is negative places himself above the object of his mockery, he is opposed to it. The wholeness of the world's comic aspect is destroyed, and that which appears comic becomes a private reaction. The people's ambivalent laughter, on the other hand, expresses the point of view of the whole world; he who is laughing also belongs to it."[12] It cannot be said that the revels in Times Square, the relentless mockery of the Rosenbergs perpetrated in the series of comedy acts that precedes their execution, meet this specification. But Coover's narrative itself goes to considerable lengths to locate itself within the world it satirizes, wary of transcendent pronouncements and cultivating the ambivalence of participation. He thus aligns himself with the spirit of carnival laughter, which Bakhtin considered to exist in an indissoluble relation to freedom. He has himself commented on the comic vision: "I tend to think of tragedy as a kind of adolescent response to the universe—the higher truth is a comic response."[13] This, in Bakhtin's terms, is a rejection of the modern attitude to laughter, that "that which is important and essential cannot be comical," in favour of the Renaissance concept of laughter: "Laughter has a deep philosophical meaning, it is one of the essential forms of the truth concerning the world as a whole, concerning history and man. . . ."[14] In order to maintain the inclusiveness of his comic vision, Coover takes great care to subvert the reflex response his material invites. An unequivocal sympathy with the victims against the establishment is resisted by a sustained distance from the Rosenbergs; the portrayal of Nixon, while acutely satiric, is also unexpectedly empathetic; Uncle Sam, too, has an appeal that conflicts with the monstrosity of his character; and the impersonal narration is given from a self-ironizing perspective within the Cold War orthodoxy, rather than the exterior perspective that straight satire would involve.

Ultimately this circle of laughter inscribes the reader too, the process of reading the book itself becoming the arena of disruption. The central strategy here, and that which has most perplexed critics, is the use of excess. It is a cumulative effect, operating principally in the impersonally narrated chapters, where it is built upon an expanding repertoire of devices. There is the manic folk speech of Uncle Sam throughout, and the whirlwind summaries of world events synchronous with and more or less related to the action of the novel. Later, there are exhaustive lists of those present at the Times Square executions (and hence in some degree culpable—a roll-call of the damned): these include lists of Hollywood celebrities, tycoons and politicians, including—alphabetically state by state—all ninety-six senators. There are slapstick and horror comic passages which continue long after their essential point has been made (the series of skits on the Death House letters, the mob hysteria during the blackout). And there are scenes which strive to exceed the limits of literary propriety, such as Nixon's sexual encounter with Ethel Rosenberg minutes before her execution, or his final initiation by Uncle Sam in the buggery scene of the epilogue. In form or content, all these devices serve the same effect, one which informs the argument of the novel as a whole. In seeking to explore and imaginatively recreate the atmosphere of Cold War hysteria Coover has deployed a technique which, in its insistence, generates an immense narrative momentum in the novel towards its denouement, analogous to that felt by America itself: "it's almost as though there is something critical about the electrocutions themselves, something down deep inside, a form, it's as though events have gone too far, as though there's an inner momentum now that can no longer be tampered with, the nation is too deeply committed to this ceremony . . ." (211). But in its excess, the narrative enacts the logic by which this momentum can compel a complicity in unsought violations: the inexorable march of the narrative exceeds the limits prescribed by convention, so that to read it at all is to be, and to experience being, coerced into transgression. The predictable and potentially trite repudiation of McCarthyist hysteria is given force and value by a method of narration that demonstrates the mechanisms involved.

Implicit in this narrative momentum is the sense of an ineluctable script to history, by which the unfolding events are motivated. It is there too in the appropriation of carnival by Uncle Sam's circus. Circus is the performance of carnival, and wherever the narrative attention turns from the circus itself to its production and reception, this difference is elucidated. It generates the concept of history as drama which finds echoes at all levels of the structure of the novel. The Rosenberg executions therefore function as the fulfilment of a script, the finale of an act in the circus of history, which satisfies America's expectations of pattern in its perceptions of itself. Such expectations are based upon the theological script of manifest destiny: "Throughout the solemn unfolding of the American miracle, men have noticed this remarkable phenomenon: what at the moment seems to be nothing more than the random rise and fall of men and ideas ... is later discovered to be ... a necessary and inevitable sequence of interlocking events, a divine code, as it were, bringing the Glad Tidings of America's election ..." (8–9). The script that governs American history is a priori, and the diversity of events must be subordinated to a pattern that will encode it. Since the meaning of the code is always subject to the interpretative will, more important than any specific pattern is the discovery of pattern as such. In the case of the Rosenbergs, the stay of execution frustrates this requirement to some degree, but provides compensations that Nixon finds quite satisfactory, however dangerous the ironies: "Friday. Sunset. The two thieves. Jews condemned by Jews. Some patterns had been dissolved by the overnight delay, it was true, but others were taking shape. Uncle Sam could not be entirely displeased, I thought" (228). It is the discovery of pattern which is important, since its meaning is always ambiguous except as an assertion of meaning itself.

Coover gives considerable attention in the novel to the ways in which this imperative is met. A chapter is devoted to the daily augmentation of history in *The New York Times,* presented as a shrine to which millions of pilgrims bow their heads each morning. The nature and value of this pilgrimage is described between quotations from the headlines on the morning before the executions. The random jumble of the headlines, a nonpolemical collection of facts, is their guarantee of objectivity, but Coover quickly shows that in presenting itself as such, the *Times* becomes a framework through which reality is sifted, and so shaped: "Yet even this extravagant accretion of data suggests a system, even mere hypotyposis projects a metaphysic. 'Objectivity' is in spite of itself a willful program for the stacking of perceptions.... Conscious or not, *The New York Times* statuary functions as a charter of moral and social order, a political force-field maker, defining meaningful actions merely by showing them ..." (191). The pilgrims draw comfort from the monumental stability of the shrine's great stone tablets, and find meaning already implicit in its assertion of order in chaos.

This function of *The New York Times* for the people of America is supplemented by *Time* magazine, whose role is to elucidate the script in the pattern. Coover personifies *Time* as the "National Poet Laureate," and elaborates his poetic credo while he surveys the scene in Times Square: "Raw data is paralyzing, a nightmare, there's too much of it and man's mind is quickly engulfed by it. Poetry is the art of subordinating facts to the imagination, of giving them shape and visibility, keeping them *personal*. . . . Some would say that such deep personal involvement, such metaphoric compressions and reliance on inner vision and imaginary 'sources,' must make objectivity impossible, and TIME would agree with them, but he would find simply illiterate anyone who concluded from this that he was not serving Truth" (320). These are familiar observations from Coover, and Larry McCaffery considers this to be "one of the most important theoretical passages in all of his work, [which] summarizes his view of how man tries to deal with disorder and randomness with the fiction-making process."[15] But McCaffery does not adequately acknowledge that the quote is given as *Time*'s formulation, not Coover's, and contains a pernicious equivocation upon the relationship of his "art" to reality. *Time*'s basic recognition of the partisan narrative that necessarily results from his shaping of the facts is consonant with the view expressed by Coover: "But yes, the human need for pattern, and language's propensity, willy-nilly, for supplying it—what happens, I think, is that every effort to form a view of the world, every effort to speak of the world, involves a kind of fiction making process. . . . There are always other plots, other settings, other interpretations."[16] But the difference between Coover's observation and *Time*'s development of it is the latter's exploitation of the power inherent in such a fiction-making process. *Time*'s acknowledgement of the subjectivity of his version of events is undercut by his pernicious claim to retain a privileged relationship with reality, to possess a "real grasp of the facts—not to mention Ultimate Truth" (320). Ultimately, *Time* does not present his reportage as fiction, and betrays a cynical, manipulative understanding of the power of his "art": "If he bursts through the scrim of phenomena and grasps the whole of tonight's events, he will celebrate them; if they overwhelm him, he will belittle them. He's a professional, after all" (329).

This perception of the power latent in historical narratives, the script-writer's opportunities in the inaccessibility of fact, is essential to both the political impetus towards the Rosenberg executions and Nixon's abortive attempt at revising the plot. Nixon's interest is first aroused by Uncle Sam's articulation of the principle in connection with the trial: "Hell, *all* courtroom testimony about the past is ipso facto and teetotaciously a baldface lie, ain't that so? . . . Like history itself—all more or less bunk, as Henry Ford liked to say. . . . Appearances, my boy, appearances! Practical politics consists in ignorin' facts! *Opinion* ultimately governs the world!" (86). Nixon is fired by the personal opportunities this idea suggests, but his fascination with it reveals a mixture of political acuteness and ideological naivety. Even as he speculates upon the latent possibilities of scripting history, he invokes the script by which it is already dominated: "What if we broke all the rules, played games with the evidence, manipulated language itself, made History a partisan ally? Of course, the Phantom was already onto this, wasn't he? Ahead of us again" (136). The concept of history as drama is obsessively dwelled upon in the Nixon chapters, drawing sustenance from the vice president's discovery of a shared thespian background with Ethel Rosenberg and his own preoccupation with performance and the public self he is always at pains to maintain and advance. His analysis of the trial dwells upon its qualities as performance, considering the merits of all the protagonists, including the Rosenbergs, as actors before an audience of jury and nation. From here the idea becomes more and more inclusive, the aspect of performance encroaching upon that of audience until the two are coextensive and universal: "Not only was everybody in this case from the Judge on down—indeed, just about everyone in the nation, in and out of government, myself included—behaving like actors caught up in a play, but we all seemed moreover to be aware of just what we were doing and at the same time of our inability, committed as we were to some higher purpose, some larger script as it were, to do otherwise" (117). Nixon's perception of the dominance of theatrical motifs at all levels of the affair leads him to the revelation that the entire episode of American history is "*a little morality play for our generation*" (119). This in turn allows the more radical perception, his recognition of its fictional nature: "And then what if, I wondered, there were no spy ring at all? What if all these characters *believed* there was and acted out their parts on this

assumption, a whole courtroom full of fantasists? . . . Whereupon the
Rosenbergs, thinking everybody was crazy, nevertheless fell for it,
moving ineluctably into the martyr roles they'd been waiting for all
along" (135).

   That Coover is able to place such subversive thoughts in the mind
of Richard Nixon is indicative of the dual function he has in the
novel. This dualism is the product of a divided consciousness Coover
is able to ground firmly in the historical model of his character. On
the one side there is his ingrained lawyer's scepticism, the sort of
analytic detachment which leaves him unconvinced by the neat narratives that surround the case: "If you walked forward through all this
data, like the journalists, like the FBI invited everybody to do, the
story was cohesive and seemed as simple and true as an epigram. . . .
But working backwards, like a lawyer, the narrative came unraveled"
(131). On the other side is the strict orthodoxy consistent with his
position as vice president of the administration that oversaw the
Rosenberg executions. His drive towards the centre of power involves a rigorous assimilation of the prevailing ideology, and the
militant anticommunism by which he made his name almost justifies
his eager appropriation of their piece of history: "even though finally
I didn't have all that much to do with the Rosenberg case itself, I
always felt that—indirectly anyway—it was my baby" (80). But the
fact that he figures hardly at all in the public record of the relevant
events allows Coover to exploit the tensions between his drive towards the centre and his felt exclusion, his observer's role, and he has
commented on his choice of Nixon as narrator in just such terms.[17]
He works this paradoxical status deep into Nixon's narrative, making
it fundamental to his character and tracing its sources right back to
childhood experiences such as his baptism at a Los Angeles revival
meeting: "I didn't really quite believe in what I was doing. It was
like being in a play and I could throw myself into the role with
intensity and conviction, but inside I was holding something back"
(525–6). Nixon is both a committed performer and an observer of his
own performance. Coover is able to use him both as the analytical
narrator of a substantial portion of the novel's material and as an
object of satire in his own right because this division is made to work
within the character himself.

In seeking an angle on the Rosenberg affair that will insinuate him into the centre, Coover's Nixon steps outside of that centre and the self by which he locates himself within it. The intimate relation between that public self and the nation's political condition means that the exposure to which the former is thus subjected also reveals the degeneracy of the latter. As Nixon turns his lawyer's eye upon the Rosenbergs, his every insight into them and the circumstances that have conspired to bring them to the chair reflects back upon the self he is obsessively remaking into the likeness of a president. His cynicism regarding all aspects of the Rosenberg case constantly works to subvert his public face and the manipulative consciousness behind it, exposing fundamental emotional repressions. So, the insight that precipitates the whole of his Sing Sing adventure is a willed projection of his own emotional isolation. Brooding over the epistolary relationship between the Rosenbergs, a parallel instance occurs to him: "Even now, I often wrote Pat letters at night for her to read in the morning. It was a way of working things out for yourself, exploring your own—then suddenly it occurred to me, what should have been obvious all along: she didn't love him. She never had . . . She had loved, yes, she was a lover, but she had no proper object for her love. I understood this" (312). In such ways Nixon's cold analysis of personal and political motivations is turned back upon the self in which it originates, the spectacle of his self-delusion being a comic juxtaposition of the contradictory perspectives within his complex identity.

By working within this divided consciousness, Coover is able to undermine the narratives of the Rosenberg prosecution and the McCarthyist atmosphere that motivated it, and even of the Rosenbergs themselves, while leaving not an alternative, revisionist narrative (which would remain, after all, a narrative) but the derelict, undermined hulk of a self, Nixon's and the nation's, held together only by self-delusion and the lust for power. Nixon as representative of the national orthodoxy is stripped bare by Nixon the cynical observer. But since the latter is only the means of securing the former position, it is the former that remains, barren but beyond the limits of his own analysis. His adherence to Cold War orthodoxy frames even those insights that explicitly deny it, so that the subversive direction in which his analytic mind carries him remains bounded by his doctrinal public self: "And then I'd realized what it was that had been bothering me: that sense that everything happening was somehow inevitable, as though it had all been scripted out in advance. But bullshit! There were no scripts, no necessary patterns, no final scenes, there was just *action,* and then *more action!* Maybe in Russia History had a plot because one was being laid on, but not here—*that was what freedom was all about!*" (362). Nixon's exposure of the "lie of purpose" (363) does not result in a liberation from his public self but in his perception of the opportunity for advancing it. When he steps outside of the script and heads for Sing Sing, it is to augment his own role in the action by rewriting it. At least this is the superficial motive: underneath the political ruthlessness unstable emotions have been aroused by the humiliations he has endured, and deeper, contradictory motives begin to surface.

The interaction between Nixon's contradictory selves and his humiliating pratfalls is the main use to which Coover puts his concept of Nixon as the clown of his circus. The clownish behaviour derives much of its force from the character of the historical original, but the main impetus of the comedy in the Nixon chapters is the combination of his series of pratfalls with an immense apparatus of self-consciousness which undertakes the assimilation of each to his created self, even as he blunders into the next. He is the only character the novel makes available for any degree of empathy, yet this intimacy is achieved through the presentation of a huge quantity of autobiographical information in ludicrously deluded self-analysis. The satiric exposure of Nixon's self-deceit does not distance the reader from him because the comedy arises from frequent glimpses of a Nixon almost wholly absent from his own narration: a Nixon who harbours unacceptable desires, feels genuine (if discreditable) emotion, shows weaknesses, naiveties and ethical uncertainties. Not *wholly* absent, because at times he is simply unable to sustain belief in his public persona: "Washington had got the obelisk, Jefferson the dome and circle, Lincoln the cube, what was there left for me? I wondered. The pyramid maybe. Something modern and Western would be more appropriate, but all I could think of were the false fronts in the old cowtowns" (265). At other, more vulnerable moments his suppressed personality is directly invoked. Coover picks up on an anecdote of Pat Nixon's (quoted as one of the novel's epigraphs), and gives it a more profound meaning for Nixon: "Beauty and the Beast, that game I used to play with Pat before we were married, my secret self. She thought it was funny, she didn't understand" (173). The comic potential of this image of Nixon as beast is exploited fully in the epilogue and in his carnivalesque rendition throughout, but Coover also uses it to intimate levels of his personality beyond the self-censored and the self-censoring, preparing the ground so that his characterization of the man is able to exceed the limits of the proba-ble: "My weakness, I knew, was an extreme susceptibility to love, to passion. This is not obvious, but it is true" (298). The intimacy with which Nixon is portrayed serves the cause of an empathetic involvement that goes well beyond the basic objectives of realist characterization. Nixon is the self-narrated representative, within the novel, of the reader subject to its narration. His self-deconstruction, exposing the series of contradictory roles by which he inscribes himself and is inscribed within his context, is vicariously that of the narrative's inscription of the reader.

Coover's Nixon, then, is a series of masks, the inadequacy of each of these indicating the existence of another behind it. The ludicrous attempt to create a statesmanlike, affable public figure is the work of the calculating, cynical politician, himself the façade of an emotionally and sexually desperate man, whose needs cover those of a pathetic self-pitying child. Nixon, with all the ragged and disreputable motives beneath his public face, is a microcosm of America, and Coover's purpose here is to explore on a psychological plane the same phe-nomena he approaches anthropologically in the impersonally narrated chapters. The unexpected sympathy for Nixon to which several reviewers have testified is a parallel to the unexpected ambivalence Coover cultivates in the novel as a whole, and Nixon's descent into himself during the Sing Sing adventure is an analogue of the commu-nal descent into dreamtime in Times Square. The stripping of the layers of his personality that occurs in his encounter with Ethel proceeds alongside repeated transformations in his motives—which, given the fantastic nature of the situation, are virtually generating the action. Initially, he is the statesmanlike vice president exchanging

ideological formulae. Behind this role the self-obsessed career politician soon becomes apparent: "I . . . moved my right foot forward
slightly and tilted my head as though expecting to be photographed.
Or rather, expecting nothing of the sort, but recalling from other
photographs that such a pose suggested alertness and vitality and
clarity of vision" (430). This strategic consciousness begins to develop
beyond its political function to serve emotional purposes: " 'Admit it,
Ethel! You've dreamed of love all your life! You dream of it now! I
know, because I dream of it, too! . . .' My God! I was amazing!"
(435). His successful transition to the emotional level allows for its
displacement by the self-pity that motivates it: " 'You won't die,
Richard! Don't be afraid!' 'Two of my brothers died!' I bawled. 'I
always thought . . . I would be *next!*' " (441). Nixon's control of the
fantasy he is living out has begun to slip, however: in a manoeuvre
that exactly mirrors the principle of excess by which the narrative
itself is driven, Nixon finds himself drawn beyond the limits of
his wish fulfilment as Ethel demands immediate sexual satisfaction,
dragging down his trousers to expose him completely in his carnal
reality. From this point Nixon recoils, and as he escapes into the
death chamber with his trousers tangled round his ankles he is already
rewriting the experience in the rhetoric of his political memoirs: "I
ducked back out of sight, reflecting that a man who has never
lost himself in a cause bigger than himself has missed one of life's
mountaintop experiences: only in losing himself does he find himself" (446).

In the parallel time scheme of events in Times Square there are
several explicit bridges to the Sing Sing narrative (the sound of
prisoners rattling their mugs against the bars, the dipping of the lights
as the dynamos are tested) which prepare for the moment when
Nixon, hiding with his pants down in the Sing Sing death chamber,
turns around to find himself standing (quite logically) on the replica
stage set in Times Square. This sudden fusion of the novel's two
narrative lines indicates the equivalence of the psychological and
anthropological levels at which they operate, but also represents
Nixon's reassimilation to the official drama. His desperate improvisation is a regathering of the paraphernalia of his constructed selves.
"Christ! I thought in a moment of numbing terror: *I can't even*

remember my name! I fought to recover that name, that self, even as I grappled with my trousers, hobbling about in a tight miserable circle, fought to drag myself back to myself, my old safe self, which was—who knows?—maybe not even a self at all, my frazzled mind reaching out for the old catchwords, the functional code words of the profession . . . " (471). The rhetoric by which he strives to regain control brings to fruition all the standard formulae of Cold War paranoia, as in his ranting articulation of the fear implicit in the domino theory: *"All we have to do is take a look at the map and we can see that if Formosa falls, the next frontier is the coast of California!"* (478–9). The scene becomes a parody of the situation during the fund crisis that had threatened his vice presidential candidacy, and echoes of the rhetorical manoeuvres of his "Checkers" speech provide a rich source of comedy: " . . . and so I came here like this tonight—and incidentally this is unprecedented in the history of American politics . . ." (474). The parallel provides him too with the device that saves him: *"I would suggest that under the circumstances, everybody here tonight should come before the American people and bare himself as I have done!"* (482).

Nixon's "pants down for America" ploy is successful, but when he oversteps the mark and demands that Uncle Sam himself comply he ruptures once more the scarcely established smoothness of the evening's performance. Trapped in the circle of Nixon's rhetoric, Uncle Sam reluctantly drops his pants, exposing the darkness beneath his façade, his identity with the Phantom, and plunging the populace into a raw encounter with their instinctual drives: "There was a blinding flash of light, a simultaneous crack of ear-splitting thunder, and then—BLACKOUT!!" (485). For the crowd, loss of the national narrative embodied in Uncle Sam unleashes all the primitive fears and carnal desires it had so effectively harnessed. "In the nighttime of the people" (486 et seq.) there occurs a communal stripping of identities parallel to Nixon's experience at Sing Sing, until the prototype of all their projected fears, like the darkness beneath Uncle Sam's pants, is exposed: "for the people in their nighttime have passed through their conventional terrors and discovered that which they fear most: each other!" (490). The exposure of this irreducible asociality is insufficient to change the course of events, however. As with Nixon, the people are unable to countenance the anarchy that has been revealed in them, and recoil into the only order available, readopting the old safe roles even in their discredited artificiality. Uncle Sam returns bearing "freedom's holy light," the nuclear glow from Yucca Flat, Nevada, and the executions proceed on cue.

While the executions are the consummation of America's renewed commitment to the script of Cold War orthodoxy, the consummation of the disaffected Nixon's personal role is achieved in the buggery scene of the epilogue. In the throes of this experience, Nixon attempts to comfort himself with just this equation of self and nation, even as the autonomy of his sceptical self is obliterated: "This is not happening to me alone, I thought desperately, or tried to think, as he pounded deeper and deeper, destroying everything, even my senses, my consciousness—but to the nation as well!" (532). Nixon's aspirations have frequently prompted him to speculate about the nature of the Incarnation: he notes from his observation of Eisenhower that it apparently requires a vacuum to fill, and self-consciously bemoans the impediment of his own self-consciousness. His final experience of the process, sodomy as the destruction of the self, by which succession to the presidency is facilitated, ends his eager conjectures: "I recalled Hoover's glazed stare, Roosevelt's anguished tics, Ike's silly smile: I should have guessed . . ." (533). Nixon's last desperate protests draw no concessions from an Uncle Sam who gleefully admits "I'se wicked, I is" (531), and he capitulates utterly to the orthodox drama, masking the pain by a wilful discovery of his love for Uncle Sam: "Of course, he was an incorrigible huckster, a sweet-talking con artist, you couldn't trust him, I knew that—but what did it matter? Whatever else he was, he was beautiful (how had I ever thought him ugly?), the most beautiful thing in all the world. I was ready at last to do what I had never done before. '*I . . . I love you, Uncle Sam!*' I confessed" (534).

Leaving Nixon huddled on the floor and bawling like a baby, Uncle Sam departs. His and the novel's parting words, "always leave 'em laughin' as you say good-bye!" (534), turn the focus of attention upon the way the reader has been situated in the narrative. A dubious complicity has been courted throughout, by means of the comic appeal of Uncle Sam himself, the accessibility of Nixon, the ubiquitous strategy of excess and the principle of carnival laughter. The reader's subjectivity is constructed by its situation within the discourse of the novel just as Nixon's identity is constructed by the roles he wants to appropriate. Nowhere is this clearer than in the carnivalesque function of laughter throughout the novel, which has been to satirize from within, resisting the illusion of transcendent perspective. Yet if satire is to remain functional as a critical tool, a distinction between laughing *at* and laughing *with* must be retained. Uncle Sam problematizes this distinction, and the argument of the novel, by turning the reader's affective implication in the narrative to unsettling effect, makes the problem explicit. *The Public Burning* ends, self-consciously, as an assertion of the moral necessity of self-consciousness: its last line is not a punch line, but an observation about punch lines.

Chapter 5

"One's Image of Oneself": Structured Identity in Walter Abish's *How German Is It*

In Abish's first novel, *Alphabetical Africa* (1974), as in most of his short pieces collected in *Minds Meet* (1975) and *In The Future Perfect* (1977), it was impossible to forget the language by which the narrative was articulated, language that both created its possibilities and severely curtailed them. The arbitrary alphabetical scheme Abish imposed on this novel kept the reader permanently aware not just of the extent to which the structure confined the narrative, but also of its *generative* influence. Each new chapter in the first half of the book, by suddenly making available a specific vocabulary, had a positive coercive force on the narrative: there was a high probability of death in chapter "D", and of the appearance of a first person singular in chapter "I". The structure, in other words, had an active role in creating the narrative that its obtrusive presence also undermined. Abish observed of the novel, "I was fascinated to discover the extent to which a system could impose upon the contents of a work a meaning that was fashioned by the form, and then to see the degree to which the form, because of the conspicuous obstacles, undermined that very meaning."[1] The fundamental principle of innovative fiction for Abish is defamiliarization, and that was the role of the abecedarian structures of *Alphabetical Africa* and much of his other writing. The defamiliarization of language is the tool of a critique which extends beyond the text to examine the self and the external world as cognitive constructs in which the structure of language is implicit, and which are therefore susceptible to an analysis that questions the neutrality of this structure. But there were limitations to this analysis as conducted in Abish's first novel: as language was both the object of attention and the means of articulating that attention, the defamiliarization of language made the latter function possible only in an illustrative sense, in which the imposed structure of the novel was analogous to the less opaque structure of language itself. The continuation of this analysis into the realm of the *effects* of structure upon self and world was foreclosed.

The essential concerns of *How German Is It* and *Alphabetical Africa* were the same: but whereas in *Alphabetical Africa* these concerns were formally constitutive—the novel presents itself as defamiliarized narrative—in *How German Is It* they inform an argument couched in terms of a representational narrative which locates it in a specific, recognizable context. In this way Abish is able to bring the formalism that motivated his language-oriented fiction within the frame of the narrative. No longer just exhibiting defamiliarized structures, he was able to elaborate the practical significance of such defamiliarization upon characters who, unlike those inhabiting *Alphabetical Africa,* were not themselves a part of the process.

The use of such a self-framing process is intimated in the novel by the quite conventional device of the novelist-protagonist. Ulrich's role as a novelist is used to develop the argument by invoking the concepts of structure and defamiliarization that preoccupy Abish. The interview he gives in Geneva, for example, provides occasion for an observation pertinent to the novel itself. Ulrich, speaking of his search for an appropriate ending to his current novel, refers to a suicide reported in the previous day's newspapers: "I mention this only because in life jumping out of a window is an end, whereas in a novel, where suicide occurs all too frequently, it becomes an explanation."[2] This echoes Abish's concern with the origin of meaning in structure (in this case, the structure of narrative). It also complements remarks on narrative structure—made in an interview—by Abish himself: "I avoid and also distrust a clearly defined and definable action, since it serves as an explanation and tends to dominate what would otherwise be a more neutral surface of information."[3] Abish has written at length about the writer's tendency to impose the tendentiousness of narrative structure upon reality in "The Writer-To-Be: An Impression of Living." In this essay he questions the ability of the prospective writer to refrain from rendering his experience into narrative: "Does the writer-to-be attach to everything he or she does a literary significance? For instance, can a writer-to-be view love as anything but a text-to-be . . . ?"[4] Ulrich, whose novels are directly autobiographical, is a paradigmatic instance of Abish's "writer-to-be." His relationships with Marie-Jean Filebra, Daphne Hasendruck and Anna Heller, as well as less intimate relationships, are all affected by his consciousness of their potential as material for future novels. He also acknowledges "a favorite habit of his—namely, attempting to view and place his personal affairs in a literary context, as if this would endow them with a clearer and richer meaning" (48).

Ulrich's awareness of his own susceptibility to the comforts of literary structure suggests that he is both vulnerable to other structures with which the novel is concerned, and receptive to the defamiliarization of those structures. Prominent among these are the frameworks within which Germany's collective guilt over the Holocaust is contained. The Holocaust is linked to Ulrich's anecdote about the suicide by the inclusion of one bizarre detail, that as the woman jumped to her death "someone on the seventh floor, or was it the eighth, sitting at his desk near the window, actually made eye contact with her" (53). Twenty-five pages later, in connection with the traffic to the Durst concentration camp, the same image recurs: "The only evidence of life on the passing trains was an occasional scarecrow face framed in the tiny cutout window of a freight car. A face whose eyes were riveted on the stationmaster, or on anyone who may have been watching the passing train, establishing a brief second of eye contact" (78). In the stare of the "scarecrow face" in the freight car the suicide's ineluctable plunge towards death is recalled. But also implied in the connection is Abish's refusal to believe that an answer to the question in this stare—"It could have been 'Where?' or 'When?' or 'Why?' " (78)—would constitute a satisfactory explanation. The various explanatory structures by which the novel's characters contain the past are similarly false to this moment: one of the refrains of the novel's last chapter runs *"Are memories only unreliable when they serve as an explanation?"* (224). The containment of the past with which the

novel is concerned is therefore linked directly to the structure of
narrative that Ulrich distrusts. And this is the same structure which
Abish resists and seeks to expose in his own fiction.

This may appear to emphasize unnecessarily the frame within
which the specifically German subject matter of the novel is placed.
The majority of the book's reviewers saw no reason to look beyond
the particulars of Abish's novel, finding them an ample source of
critical observations and, usually, approval. Discussion did not centre
upon the general principles at work in the dealings of the novel's
characters with their Nazi heritage, but on the accuracy and fairness
of this representation of the German people. But such a critical
response appears to be itself driven by a need to normalize the novel,
to reduce it to the familiar. Abish himself was dissatisfied with the
disproportionate critical attention given to his book's function as
social critique: "he complains that some of his readers and critics
'have failed to understand' his novel. 'They cannot see the element
of play in the book. The "history" is too close.' "[5] This element of
play is the subversion by which Abish seeks to contain the specifically
German material of the book within the larger narrative it is intended
to serve; a purpose made abundantly clear by the degree of resistance
Abish marshals against the transparent narration of this subject matter.
In a variety of ways he strives to make his narrative artificial, and to
that extent opaque, defamiliarized. The novel is permeated with
obstructions to unselfconscious narrative: these are not to be ignored
or dismissed as mannerisms, as they were by the majority of reviewers, but acknowledged as a means of distancing the characters and
action from the reader and interposing the substantial presence of the
narrative itself. The most general of these devices is the use of short
discrete sections, often single paragraphs, sometimes single sentences,
without strict regard for logical relations of narrative time or consistency of reference from one section to the next. The effect of this
"intersticed prose" has been discussed in a broader context by Edward
Marcotte: "The narrational hiatus is a device for projecting the nonlinear into a medium heretofore dominated by temporal continuity.
The emphasis on discrete segments disrupts this continuity, creating a
shift from the temporal to the spatial."[6] A shift of emphasis, in *How
German Is It,* from the unfolding events in Wurtenberg, Geneva,

Brumholdstein and the East Frisian Islands to the general conditions which govern them all, viewed as they are now more side by side than consecutively. At the same time, Abish maintains a strong element of suspense, of underlying mystery, which allows one critic to describe the novel as a "nightmarish detective story."[7] The energy of this suspense, however, is transferred from the action to the analysis and it is only through the unification of these two (quite explicitly, as psychoanalysis) that the novel reaches its denouement.

The narration that oversees these intersticed segments both articulates the subject matter and, through a series of self-interrogations on issues ranging from narrative minutiae to general thematic preoccupations, initiates and directs that articulation. Some of these questions and related imperatives ("Answer. Answer immediately") are italicized, providing grounds for discerning, as Douglas Messerli does, the additional framing of the narrative effected by two narrative voices.[8] Actually, since there is no incompatibility between the italicized interlocutions and the rest there is no reason to suppose the italics to imply anything other than a greater degree of urgency in the narration. But the urgency is directed towards the general concerns of the frame rather than the events of the narrative, so the effect remains one of distancing those events. This interrogation, in its emphasis on the *locution* of the narrative—the imperatives, "answer," "repeat," etc., address the telling rather than the told—clearly direct attention towards an argument situated at one remove from the narrative itself. It is the exploration of the role of structure, rather than the story of Ulrich itself, which is the novel. Its critique of the post-war "new Germany" does not provide the significance of the novel, but the material in which significance is to be sought. The narrative frame is not subordinate to the story itself but rather dominates and leads it.

An example of this is the emphasis upon persistent and unanswered questions, which originates in the narrative frame but soon bleeds into the narrative itself. Ulrich himself is a compulsive questioner— "My God, he does have many questions today, doesn't he, said Egon. What will he want to know next?" (237)—and he is also aware of the characteristic lack of answers with which questions are met in the novel: "Ulrich refrained from asking her any questions . . . he might have feared that his questions would only lead to further questions"

(173). In conversations throughout the novel the unanswered question becomes a motif, so that exchanges occur in which question is met with question until a tacit agreement is reached not to pursue the answers further:

> You get upset, and you slap her around. Is that true?
> Are you asking me these questions for your next article in *Treue?*
> Must you drive this fast? She asks.
> Do you believe her?
> Can't we pull up somewhere for a minute and look at the landscape? It's so beautiful over here. And when he obligingly stops the car, she embraces him and carefully plants a kiss on his lips, a kiss that he accepts as an article of faith. (135)

The narrative draws attention to itself as narrative in other ways, not least of which is the emphasis upon words throughout. In dialogue, communication repeatedly breaks down with an inquiry such as "are you sure you have the right word?" (183) and this questioning of language is a feature of the impersonal narration itself: "Is that the right word?" (174). At certain points disproportionate attention is given to a particular word via phrases like "the key word here is 'sniffed' " (128), and one of the pictures in the colouring book whose message Ulrich struggles to decipher depicts on a garage wall the graffito "DAS WORT IST EIN MOLOTOV COCKTAIL!" (178).

There are also discreet but persistent displays of self-consciousness. "This is an introduction to a window on the fifth floor" (31) begins one section; at other points the urbane address to the reader is punctuated by the self-negating phrase "Absolutely no irony intended" (124). This sort of self-reference is sustained at a level sufficient to ensure the continuous presence of the narrating text before the reader. A derivative of it is the extensive use of repetition throughout the novel, which is not confined to the direct echoing of phrases but extends as far as a slightly skew repetition of the first two sections of part two, "The Idea of Switzerland," at the beginning of part three, "Sweet Truth." The slight differences suspend the reader in a hauntingly incomplete familiarity with the text, thus introducing at a higher level one of Abish's central concerns—"the familiar"—

while simultaneously helping assert the primary significance of these concerns. A similar effect is produced by the enigmatic image of "a horse standing in a lake, in one or two feet of water, with its muscular erect bareback rider wearing a visored military cap and looking into the camera's lens" (201) which appears in Ulrich's colouring book, among Rita's photographs (where the rider is identified as the man who shot at Helmuth) and on the cover of the novel itself. By transgressing narrative levels this recurrent image forces the narrative structure upon the reader's consciousness, but at the same time it augments the aura of mystery in the novel. The reader's involvement is simultaneously intensified and abstracted from the story itself, allowing Abish to elaborate an argument both urgent and detached.

Speaking of the function of narrative voice in the novel, Douglas Messerli observes that "The reader of Abish's fiction finds himself less interested in the characters as personages than as illustrations reflected by the authorial voice. In short, the author steals his fiction from his own creations, so to speak."[9] The perception of characters as "illustrations," created by and for the purposes of an argument cast in terms of the authorial narration, indicates the limited role they have in the novel. *How German Is It* does not efface its narrative or present an uncompromised narrative world. But neither does it adopt subversive strategies in anything like the rigorous manner of *Alphabetical Africa,* and so its formal properties cannot bear anything like the burden of significance they have in that book. Abish's motives are less direct, involving both a resistance to narrative verisimilitude and a necessary appeal to just such a developed narrative context. The operation of these two impulses in tandem ensures that the narrative content cannot be accepted as simply itself, but as the field in which something else (the abstract intellectual structure of the book) is signified. Abish's use of subtly defamiliarized narrative allows substantial development of the story while nonetheless establishing it as less an end in itself than the occasion of a larger argument.

The argument of the novel, then, is abstracted from and more fundamental than the German narrative through which it is presented. While this has not been generally recognized, however, it is possible to overstate the case, as Richard Martin does: "*How German Is It* deals with Ulrich Hargenau's search for himself within himself, within his national past and present. In terms of Abish's own predominant interests, however, the novel is an extended examination of the familiar in its absorption of the unfamiliar, and of responses to apparent perfection. In both contexts Germany is simply an association, a pretext."[10] To suggest that Germany, and the idea of Germany, is not important in the novel is to disregard both its dominance in the narrative and the greater part of the novel's force; even if this was defensible the result would be a devaluation of Abish's achievement. The specifically German elements of the narrative and the characters who generate it should be seen as functions of Abish's general abstract concerns, but not as incidental for that reason. In writing of Germany's assimilation of its past Abish has chosen a compelling and frequently addressed issue (the familiarity of which is itself pertinent to his designs, as I shall argue later). He develops his characters and action with a novelistic attention, not as the ad hoc associations that might dress another type of discourse. The strength of fiction lies in its ability to view concrete details as having general significance, not for the sake of the generality in its own right, but for the illumination of the concrete and particular; the importance of Abish's abstract explorations derives from the importance of the circumstances in which they are manifest, so that to downgrade the specifics of his narrative is to trivialize the whole enterprise. The general and the theoretical are the motivating force of the novel, but their significance derives from their illumination of the relations of its characters to each other and their shared past, and the relation of the narrative itself to the idea of Germany. The same principles that informed Abish's earlier works are operating in *How German Is It,* but here they resonate with the particularity of a sustained narrative situation.

The issues addressed by *How German Is It* are subsumed in an argument relating the concepts of structure and identity: the narrative is driven by the difficulties in evolving a coherent self-image in Germany after the war, in a climate where the wholesale recantations of Nazi ideology are defied by the powerful structure of the cultural heritage within which it grew. The interaction of structure and identity is apparent on several levels: the impositions of the German past upon the post-war national self-image, the new Germany; the ambivalent response of the individual to a family structure contami-

nated with Nazism; the individual's orientation towards the national
past; and the individual's location within the new Germany—the
national self-image regarded here as itself a determining structure.
The Germany Abish presents is further pertinent to the argument in
the extremity of its national preoccupation with order and stability, a
deference to structure that consolidates its influence upon individual
identity in the new Germany, as in the old. Characters in the novel
also devote a great deal of time to delineating their self-images within
the structures of their peers, work relations, political sympathies,
sexual entanglements, to the notable neglect of direct interpersonal
contact. In general terms, the central concept of "the familiar" speci-
fies a stable relationship between self-image and contextual structure.
The process of defamiliarization which for Abish is the raison d'être
of innovation is enacted in the plot, where the characters are confronted with the structures within which they locate themselves and
the stability of these relationships is undermined. Abish has noted that
"forms, systems, structures, constrictive and otherwise, are not alien
to life or literature. We simply have not developed an orientation
in literature that would acknowledge them."[11] Here just such an
orientation is attempted through the defamiliarization of the form of
the novel, a disruptive foregrounding of the narrative structure that
alerts the reader to the implications of analogous disruptions *within*
the narrative.

The novel's concern with structured identity is advertised in its
title, which insists upon examining everything in relation to the
structural context, Germany, and also the existence of such a structure, the "German," which is itself a national identity contingent
upon historical structures. Its epigraph quotes Jean-Luc Godard in
terms that confirm the general scope of the novel's analysis: "What is
really at stake is one's image of oneself." The short first part of the
novel, "The Edge of Forgetfulness," is devoted mainly to the question of national identity—the critical concept that combines the
functions of structure and structured. The end of the chapter discloses
that it is Ulrich himself who is self-consciously "returning from the
edge of forgetfulness" (9), a return to Germany in order to confront
and examine the formative structures by which he implicitly defines
himself. That Ulrich is situated as himself German, rather than an

outsider, is Abish's major revision of his earlier story, "The English Garden," in which the argument of *How German Is It* is anticipated.[12] This revision is crucial for two reasons: because it provides scope for exploring the protagonist's own problematic relation to the general question of German-ness; and because the motivation it attaches to the explanatory tendencies inherent in Ulrich's vocation as a writer, and in the narrative itself, makes such explanations double-edged and self-cancelling.

Ulrich's self-image is dominated by the structure of personal relationships: his muted antagonism towards his brother; his estrangement from his anarchist wife, Paula; his ambivalence towards his (nominal) father. But all of these also imply larger structural forces: Ulrich equates Helmuth with the new Germany, without specifying his own position with regard to either; Paula's Einzieh Group is a pure negation of the new Germany, but also fails to define Ulrich, who has both accepted and betrayed its cause; his father implies both the Nazism he espoused until 1942 and, in his conspiracy and execution, its repudiation. Ulrich's vocation as a writer similarly supports the argument, itself involving structural impingements upon his identity. His work is specifically autobiographical, and his evasive answer when confronted with the fact indicates the structural function it serves: "Existence does not take place within the skin, he replied, quoting Brumhold" (18). Ulrich does not deny that his novels are a structuring of his experience, but rather asserts that this has already occurred in the act of conceiving of one's own existence, as Abish himself makes clear when expanding upon the same subject in interview: "Heidegger refers to being as something that does not take place within the skin. Existence, itself, means to stand outside oneself."[13] The process of self-definition through literary form that Ulrich conducts in his books, each one a subordination of a period of his life to the structure of a novel, is the way he stands outside himself and is a product of the literary perspective by which, however self-consciously, he frames all his experience. But his recent exile and the continued threat of death under which he lives in the wake of his betrayal of the Einzieh Group effect an almost universal defamiliarization of his defining structures, injecting into even the most innocuous circumstances an element of mystery, of undefinable menace. As a result, he is unable to locate the certainties of his relationships or the stability of his situation. This leaves his identity in a state of flux, subject to continuous self-examination, just as the extension of the process of defamiliarization into the impersonal narrative creates the sense of narratorial irresolution that powers the novel's explorations.

The methodology of Abish's analytical argument is best understood by returning to the structure with which Abish was first preoccupied, language. The relation of identity and structure can here be translated into the structuralist distinction between parole and langue, the figure and ground of language. In *Alphabetical Africa* and his language-oriented short pieces Abish was essentially creating texts that act out their own semiological self-analysis, demonstrating through the process of defamiliarization both the interdependence of the signifier and the signified, and the contingency of signification. If language in these works is analogous to the experience of social and cultural structures in *How German Is It,* then this too can be seen as the object of semiological analysis: the continuity of Abish's concerns can therefore be expressed as an evolution from linguistic to cultural semiology. Rather than defamiliarizing the language that defines his narrative, Abish seeks to defamiliarize the cultural structures by which the characters in his narrative are defined and define themselves. While in his earlier work the effect is to undermine the autonomy of the narrative, refuting the necessary logic of its representations by the conspicuous presence of the linguistic structure within which they are articulated, in this novel the identities of characters, communities, and a nation are exposed to their contingency by the defamiliarization of their unacknowledged formative structures. This approach has an obvious precedent in Roland Barthes' *Mythologies,* where the demystifying set-piece analyses of cultural phenomena serve the same broad purpose—Abish's "defamiliarization" being equivalent to Barthes' preferred term, "semioclasm."[14] The novel in fact contains one set piece that would hardly be out of place in Barthes' book— the analysis of Egon and Gisela's cover photograph for the magazine *Treue.* The cover, which becomes an icon not only for Egon and Gisela themselves but also for Franz, is treated as a matrix of signs articulating the exemplary new German lifestyle of its subjects in a form more concise and more powerful than the accompanying article

can achieve: "In a sense, everything in the eight-page article on Egon
and Gisela in the magazine *Treue* is already conveyed and analysed on
the front cover" (126). The photograph is minutely described, along
with a commentary which both articulates the correct response to
each significant detail and, in exposing that signifying function, subverts it:

> Egon, in a double-breasted white gabardine suit, leaning against
> the car. To be precise, he was casually (incidentally, this casualness
> cannot be overemphasized) leaning against the left front fender of
> his (their?) white Mercedes convertible. . . . Gisela . . . bending
> slightly at the waist—gracefully, to be sure, in order to adjust the
> collar on Dumas, their giant schnauzer. . . . She is only doing this
> because the dog's collar requires adjustment. . . . As for Egon:
> there is something to be said in favor of such a casual (that
> word again) indifference to the distinct possibility that he might
> irreparably stain his white suit with car grease. . . . Gisela's swept-
> back blonde hair, the hairdo emphasizing a sleekness, a sexual
> sharpness. . . . The viewer cannot remain unaware of the tasteful
> arrangement of all these possessions and of the combination of
> colors: the yellow villa, the red flowers, the black trousers, and the
> black dog. Colors that are and always have been quintessentially
> German—Schwartz, Rot, Gold. (125–9)

The cover photograph is the focus of a semiological analysis which
also embraces the magazine article itself and its accompanying photographs, defining it as "essentially an attempt to package (this is the
favored American expression) the two of them or, for that matter, an
attempt to package Germany" (128). Surrounding and interrupting
this is a countertext in which the elements suppressed by the signifying structure are exposed: Egon's weak and petulant pout, Gisela's
gaunt, angular features and hysterical tendencies; Egon's intimacy
with his secretary and subsequent affair with the photographer Rita;
Gisela crouching miserably in the corner of her room. But for Egon
and Gisela as much as for the magazine's readership, the cover's
complex of signals establishes an identity—"It's us," (133)—which
both of them badly need, and which they cannot extrapolate from
the multiple, conflicting evidences of their actual lives.

The magazine cover is a text in the same way that for Barthes the face of Garbo or a wrestling match or a striptease is a text; the analytical process is the same. But the target is more specific for Abish than for Barthes—for Abish the impositions of covert signifying structures are to be considered with particular respect to their consequences for identity, here the self-images of Egon and Gisela and the new Germany. And the context is crucially different: it occurs within the frame of a fiction, the narration of which is insistently, even obsessively, analytical, so that the argument embraces both the narrative and the narration, and issues raised in one reflect upon the other. Another clearly defined semiological text in the novel is the colouring book, "entitled, *Unser Deutschland*" (176). This defamiliarizes the defining function served by the representative scenes such a colouring book would normally contain by including scenes with unexpected associations: along with unexceptional pictures of airports and *autobahns,* it depicts a traffic accident, a dilapidated railroad freight car, and a man held at gunpoint by masked women. The book, sent to Ulrich by Daphne, presents a defamiliarized Germany within which he must locate himself, as is implied by the handwritten messages— "Wo bist du denn?" "Have you really given up the search?" (177, 179)—that Ulrich finds so cryptic. Aside from the set-piece analyses that only a clearly defined text will allow, the semioclasmic function of the narrative can be traced through the novel at every level. Many of the narrative's italicized single line questions and comments, such as *"Could everything be different?"* (176) or *"What everyone knows"* (183), address themselves directly to the defamiliarization of the everyday by defining it as such and bringing its self-evidence into question.

The ostensible focus of defamiliarization in the novel is the vast repression of the unbroachable subject of Nazism, and in particular personal relations to it, in German everyday life. The workings of this repression are highlighted in particular by the function of the weather as a safe alternative conversational subject. This first occurs at the very beginning of part two, and the convention is immediately defamiliarized by a casual indiscretion that invokes associations far less innocuous:

A glorious German summer.
Oh, absolutely.

Easily the most glorious summer of the past thirty-three years.
Thirty-three years? Certainly, he agreed. (11)

The narrative provides its own commentary, "It is safe to conclude
that people discussing the weather may be doing so in order to avoid
a more controversial subject" (11), which infects all future mention
of the weather with a conspiratorial undertone, reinforced by the
urgent italicized narrative voice seizing upon such remarks: "*Repeat:
Looks like another fine day?*" (20). An ability to respond correctly to
the weather takes on an ironic moral force, for to fail is to rupture
the ordered surface of life and acknowledge a reality beyond the
signifiers of normality: "Could it be that an inner turmoil, an absence
of serenity, an unresolved entanglement, self-doubt, self-hatred may
be due to nothing more serious than a person's inability to appreciate
the idyllic weather?" (16). A social convention, then, is not only
treated as the mediating structure between a nation's self-image and
its history, but also as an impingement upon individual personality.

From the equation of Abish's "defamiliarization" with Barthes'
"semioclasm," it will be clear that Abish's equivalent of Barthes'
"natural," by which he describes the confusion of myth with self-
evident truth,[15] is "the familiar." It is a concept to which Abish has
given attention outside his fiction, in a paper entitled "On Aspects of
the Familiar World as Perceived in Everyday Life and Literature."[16]
With discreetly self-deprecating humour, Abish has a version of this
paper presented in *How German Is It* in the form of Anna Heller's
discussion with her school class. This discussion successfully blends a
concise articulation of the essential elements of Abish's concept with
a series of ironic modulations created by the narrative context. So
Anna chooses at random an illustration of the fundamental qualities
of the familiar: "Now the street below is, as I have already pointed
out, familiar, but it is not the same street we saw yesterday or the
street we will see tomorrow. It is always changing, only most of the
time we pay no attention to the changes. . . . We are not surprised by
them. One might even venture to say that the familiar is reassuring"
(119). The familiar, then, is a subjective assimilation of variable details
to a reassuringly stable interpretative structure. The street Anna refers
to, however, is later to crumble, exposing the unassimilable fact of

the mass grave on which it is built. The familiar involves a process of repression or exclusion as well as assimilation, and the relationship between the familiar and the known is therefore problematic. The past is known, but in the process of familiarization certain elements, those whose significance is most unsettling, can remain unassimilated. For Anna the past is familiar, but the narrow horizons within which she defines it suggest a repression that undermines and ironizes her elementary reasoning: "Now, if we think about the past, if we think about anything that happened in the past: yesterday, the day before, a week ago, aren't we to some extent thinking about something that we consider familiar?" (121). The revelation of the mass grave enacts the rediscovery of the unfamiliar within the familiar, and Anna's response to it demonstrates her determination to resist the process of defamiliarization: "She said she didn't want to talk about it. She said that a lot of people were killed in the war, and that it was very sad" (138). But Anna is unable to prevent the subversion of the familiar in her own life, and in the light of the disintegration of her affair with Helmuth, the hints in the text are enough to characterize her prepossession with the familiar as itself evidence of a crisis of defamiliarization: "But why would Miss Anna Heller spend so much time discussing the familiar, unless she had some doubts, some reservations regarding the familiar, day-to-day events of her life. . . . If we ever forget something that is familiar, then, quite likely, someone will remind us, saying: You forgot to say good morning. You forgot to kiss me" (121).

Essential to the familiar is the function of repetition, by which experience is transformed, in fact or memory, from the singularity of the unfamiliar into a recognizable component of given contextual structures. At the same time, repetition functions in the narrative as a defamiliarizing force, its redundancy drawing attention to otherwise quite unexceptional, familiar details and implying an element of the unfamiliar in them. This process parallels Ulrich's own experience of radical defamiliarization and also raises an issue that renders the familiar, and therefore identity, far less stable: "Sometimes he felt as if his brain had become addicted to repetitions, needing to hear everything repeated once, then twice in order to be certain that the statement was not false or misleading. He found himself repeating what he

intended to do next, even though he would be the first to acknowledge that repetition precluded the attainment of perfection or, as
the American thinker Whitehead put it: Perfection does not invite
repetition" (15). The concept of perfection, then, is incompatible
with familiarity since repetition destroys its unity and singularity.
There is one exception acknowledged in the novel: "their love of
nature . . . a satisfying almost unseen backdrop to their existence. Yet,
something one can label as being both familiar and perfect" (133).
Only nature can be both familiar and perfect since the familiar (as
implied by Barthes' equivalent term) is a subjective artifice aspiring to
the natural. But attainment of the supreme order of perfection in
human, cultural and social structures is impeded by the need to
rehearse, to repeat at every level; to approach the natural by way of
the familiar.

The problem of the inimical qualities of perfection and familiarity
is combatted by Egon and Gisela and their new German lifestyle,
which is "Clearly an attempt to achieve perfection" (125), by a
concerted strategy against familiarity: "It is all there . . . the innate
German upper- and upper-middle class instinct to combine what is
essentially 'perfection' with the 'menacing' " (127). Menace is the
attempt to use repetition both ways: as an agent of naturalization,
and, by means of its clear and aggressive signalling of its coercive
force, also the agent of an irreducible, sinister unfamiliarity. The
more rigid the structure, the more extreme the menace: absolute
violence is intrinsic to absolute order. The exaggerated veneration of
order that characterizes the novel's new Germany leads the inhabitants of Brumholdstein to a vigorous repression of the Nazi past that
has resurfaced with the mass grave and disrupted their collective self-
image. But this veneration of order was also fundamental to the rise
of Nazism itself. Abish relates in interview an anecdote that highlights
the implicit totalitarianism in the equation of stability with moral
value: "Goethe, I believe, condemned Kleist for being unstable. He
also helped ruin Kleist's career. Sure enough, Kleist shortly thereafter
committed suicide as if to prove Goethe correct. It's hardly surprising
that Goethe became a culture hero for generations of Germans who
above everything else dreaded disorder, and equated order with a
moral rational development."[17] The importance of this same value in

the new Germany is articulated by Egon in his interview for *Treue:*
"Clearly the Einzieh Group intends to overthrow our system of
government by destroying Germany's newly acquired harmony. . . .
If anything can be said to represent the new Germany, it is the wish,
the desire, no, the craving to attain a total harmony" (130–1). The
Einzieh Group here, like the Baader-Meinhof Gang to which it
alludes, takes on a totemic significance wholly disproportionate to its
actual strength—"Yes, the German gift for presenting an exaggerated
menace to the prevailing order" (199)—which serves as a foil to the
ominous invocation of a "total harmony." The oppressive potential
still inherent in this substitution of order for morality is apparent in
the police film on terrorism provoked by the Einzieh Group: "In
order to clarify, to make evident a terrorist threat, the film has to
distort, fabricate and often lie. But no matter how great these flaws
are, the need for the film is self-evident. . . . [We need] greater
freedom to respond to the terrorist threat with measures we consider
appropriate. Measures that would not necessarily receive support
from the general public or the press" (243–4).

The German national identity is the key to all other instances of
the relation of structure and identity in the novel, because here the
identity in question is formed by the structure of the national history
as perceived by its citizens and is itself a structure by which those
citizens define themselves. Brumholdstein, located on the site of the
Durst concentration camp, is a literalization of the foundations upon
which the new German identity has been built, and its inhabitants are
representative of the new German consciousness. It exists in an un-
easy relationship with the past, with the neighbouring old town of
Daemling and with Durst itself. The past is not entirely effaced, but
contained by a strict demarcation of its relevance to the present, as in
the careful emphasis with which the subject of Durst is treated in the
books in Brumholdstein's library: "Durst, the former railroad juncture
built in 1875, enlarged in 1915, and further enlarged in 1937 shortly
after the Durst labor camp was constructed. The critical date for
Durst remains 1956, when the giant bulldozers arrived to level the
camp and huge trailer trucks came to haul away the gas ovens and
other machinery for scrap metal" (81). When Brumholdstein's main
street collapses to reveal this carefully contained past in the mass

grave, the townspeople rehearse a series of manoeuvres that represent
the new Germany struggling to sustain its self-image in the face of
defamiliarization. In the immediate wake of the incident there is a
frenzy of self-justifications and evasions of responsibility that address
the collapse itself, but obviously recall the response provoked by the
original revelation of the death camps: "Things like that were bound
to happen. They could happen anywhere. No one was really to
blame. . . . My people tell me that they expected this would happen.
Well, I ask you, why the hell didn't they do something to prevent it?
. . . I reported it, but no one came" (136).

The mass grave's unequivocal message is resisted by a desperate
search for alternative interpretations. This is not exactly an attempt to
refute the obvious but a defensive recourse to doubt, an undermining
of the authority of the past by considering its relics as ambiguous
evidence of a lost narrative, and so diminishing its actuality. It is
worth noting that more than one critic, conditioned in textual
scepticism, failed to detect any irony here: "On the other hand, can
anyone really rule out the possibility, remote as it might appear, that
these people were not inmates of the camp but Germans killed in air
raids, or killed by Americans, or killed by the inmates after they had
been released. . . . It was unlikely, improbable, but could not be ruled
out" (192). The authorities of Brumholdstein busy themselves with
diversionary questions of administration, as a way of dealing with the
problem without engaging its significance; this response is also a
prioritization of order that effectively reasserts the self-image that has
been subverted. But even the administrative details cannot help but
collide with the suppressed past, creating ironic dilemmas such as the
question of a memorial inscription for the exhumed corpses: "would
a simple line or two suffice? Perhaps: Men and women, inmates of
Durst. Identity unknown. Cause of death, unknown. May they rest
in peace" (192).

That the unassimilated history of the Holocaust constitutes a continuing threat to German national identity, a destabilization of the
fundamental structure of new German society, is indicated by the
desperation with which its textuality is seized upon, allowing exactly
the scepticism towards signifying structures that is avoided with regard to the national identity itself: "But how reliable is this evidence,

these articles by former inmates or by writers who specialize in the sensational, in the outrageous? . . . Did this really occur or have these photographs been carefully doctored, ingeniously concocted simply in order to denigrate everything German? It would not be the first time" (190–1). At one level, the narrative rehearses a quite conventional satiric demolition of this hypocrisy; but it also unsettles that perspective by admitting the extremity of the situation for the individual's self-image in the new Germany: "lampshades from human skin, soap produced from human fat. It's too much. It's more than one can bear" (191). If it is just "more than one can bear" that Germany should be accused of such things, the satiric potential is brought into play. But if it is unbearable for the individual that these things be true of the nation within the structure of which he or she has achieved self-definition, then the dominant impression is that of the impossible double bind in which the self-image of a generation of Germans is caught: to deny the past, or to destroy the self.

Ulrich's own self-image is also vulnerable to the unassimilated past, but the problem for him is encapsulated in his relation to his father. Ulrich von Hargenau's conspiracy against the Nazi regime provides several points of comparison with Ulrich's own involvement with the Einzieh Group, but the equivalence between their conspiratorial roles is complex and ambiguous. Clearly the interpretation chosen by the group was misguided: "Ulrich von Hargenau, the elder, had died—or so it would appear—without divulging the names of his fellow conspirators. So why couldn't they expect Ulrich Hargenau, the younger, to follow his example?" (22). Ulrich's betrayal of the group at the Einzieh trial is the occasion of a damning contrast with his father by *Der Spiegel,* which "depicted Ulrich and Paula in the most unflattering terms, devoting a good part of the article to a comparison of his *cowardly* actions to the *selfless* conduct of his father in 1944" (34). But Ulrich's father was a Nazi before he was ever a conspirator, and his betrayal of the Nazi cause might equally parallel Ulrich's betrayal of the Einzieh Group. The ambiguous significance of Ulrich's emulation of his father encapsulates the contradictions of German responses to the war. As a conspirator against Nazism Ulrich von Hargenau has a certain status: "It is no secret that in some circles his father, Ulrich von Hargenau, is considered a hero. Hargenau? Of

course. The fellow who was executed in '44. No need to say more"
(4). But only in some circles; the problem of the national response to
such a role lies in the uncertain identity of the enemy against which
he conspired. The new Germany cannot dissociate itself from the
nation under Nazism, as the issue of Würtenburg's war memorial
makes clear: "There were at least six Hargenaus, naturally all officers,
who died in World War I, and another half a dozen (Ulrich von
Hargenau's name not included) whose names were carved into the
large slab of marble now placed, after a heated debate, behind the
Schottendorferkirche, a somewhat out of the way part of the city,
considered at the time by many as a more suitable spot for a World
War II monument" (19). If it is necessary to honour the nation's
dead, however discreetly, then the continuity of national identity has
been acknowledged, and this memorial must exclude as traitors those
who acted against it.

Ulrich himself acknowledges the ambiguity of his father's status in
his psychoanalysis at the end of the novel, but then reveals that he
cannot be his father's son, the date of his execution making this
impossible. He continues to call him father because he does not want
to know his true father: "I can't deny that I am afraid to find out
who my father may be . . . afraid to discover what role he played
during the war" (250). The legacy of Ulrich von Hargenau is prefera-
ble not because it is unsullied (that option is unavailable) but because
it is ambiguous. Ulrich recognizes that he may have sought to construct his own identity by playing the ambiguities of his personal
heritage against each other: "Is it possible that I agreed to work with
the group because I wanted a role that would, in a certain respect,
parallel the role my father played in '44? He was not cut out to be a
conspirator, and I . . . I let down the group. Was that a deliberate act
on my part?" (251).

The parallel between Ulrich and his father makes the Einzieh
Group fundamental to his identity, so that his condition since the
trial (at which point his father's function as a model is cut off by his
execution) is one of comprehensive defamiliarization. This psychological causation is reinforced by a literal consequence of the trial, the
constant threat of death under which he lives: "frequently, two or
three times a week, he received a letter from some anonymous person

who appeared to hate him with a greater passion and intensity than he had ever been able to hate anyone" (17–18). As the novel progresses, this menace itself becomes tied up with his current relationship with Daphne. The importance of this relationship is not apparent until the novel's denouement, but it is prepared for by the association between Daphne and the first Einzieh bombing of the narrative: "The image of the explosion and their making love were linked or connected by the date on which both events had taken place, and possibly by the conviction he always had that nothing is what it first appears to be" (42). The event that shocks Ulrich into seeking help through hypnosis is the third explosion, the dynamiting of the bridge to Gänzlich minutes before he would have passed over it. But the significance of the event for him is less the proximity of death (which he has already experienced twice) but its defamiliarization of his purpose for being there, his motives for seeking out Daphne: "I wasn't really going out of my way to see her. But the dynamited bridge made all the difference in the world. I asked myself, why was I going to see her? Was it simply because I found myself in possession of her address? Or because I wanted to clarify if she had really, as I've been led to suspect, infiltrated the Einzieh Group . . ." (251).

Why this should be of such interest to him can only be answered in terms of identity. If Daphne's identity during their relationship was structured by her assumed role as a member of the Einzieh Group, and Ulrich's own involvement was the product of a self-image constructed according to his father's equivocal precedent, then what appeared to be a spontaneous personal relationship turns out to be simply a moment of circularity in a complex of structures. In going to visit Daphne he had sought to verify this radically defamiliarizing illustration of the epiphenomenal nature of identity. Ulrich has until this point attempted to locate himself within, or between, his defining structures, without allowing them to actually define him. The sequence of transitory relationships he forms with women conform to this pattern of structures solicited and then rejected: "Everytime I followed a woman in the past I hoped that it would turn out to be you. What would happen now, Marie-Jean asked him shortly before they separated, if the woman turned out to be me?" (28). He steps out of the structure of these relationships by framing each within the structure of a novel; similarly he escapes from the new Germany by joining the Einzieh Group; from that structure by his betrayal; from the possibility of his true father by emulating his nominal father; and from his nominal father in the final scene by acknowledging his uncertain parentage. Underlying this flight from self-definition is his fear of the German past it must ultimately acknowledge. In seeking out Daphne he had begun to confront the futility of this flight and to desire the relative calm of acquiescence in the hegemony of that past. Under hypnosis, Ulrich concedes the ineluctable power of the structure of the past over his identity: "And Ulrich, who felt pleasantly relaxed, slowly raised his arm, perhaps for no better reason than a desire not to impede the hypnosis, or a wish to please the doctor. For no other reason. . . . He knew, he was convinced, he was positive that he was not a good hypnotic subject as he opened his eyes, with his right hand raised in a stiff salute" (252).

The inevitability of this diagnosis, and indeed Ulrich's acquiescence in it, reintroduce the question of explanations and the suspicion with which they are regarded by both Ulrich and Abish. The hypnosis produces an entirely familiar explanation of the new Germany, but Abish refuses it—precisely by identifying the appeal of that familiarity to Ulrich himself: the uncertain degree and nature of his collaboration in his own hypnosis discredits the synthetic revelation it offers. An earlier scene has prepared for this self-negating resort to explanatory cliché, when Gisela conducts a psychological test by making Ulrich select from a tray of objects: "Among the shells and coins he spotted a tiny swastika, perhaps the one that his father had at one time worn in his buttonhole" (212). Ulrich, in an act of excruciating self-consciousness, performs the repudiation of his father's Nazi past by "selecting the tiny eraser that was encased in a plastic case made to resemble a bomb" (213). His gawkish symbolism empties the gesture of its ostensive meaning, allowing Abish both to invoke and to undermine the explanation towards which his narrative inevitably tends. Abish has insisted upon this point in interview:

> There is no wrapup to *How German Is It*. That's why I wrote the book. That's why I picked Germany. Because, to this day, hardly anyone can mention Germany, or write about Germany, without

feeling the necessity to . . . "wrap up Germany." Everything German necessitates an explanation and, of course, it is invariably the same familiar explanation. I suspect that one brings up the subject of Germany only in order to arrive at the explanation. To me the literary challenge was to see to what degree it would be possible to write about Germany without fulfilling those obligations. The ending is highly charged because it is denied the explanation that will defuse it.[18]

The novel ends with a rhetorical question: "Is it possible for anyone in Germany, nowadays, to raise his right hand, for whatever the reason, and not be flooded by the memory of a dream to end all dreams?" (252). By falling into cliché the implied assertion empties itself of content, betraying an evasion of its own, a failure to confront the past squarely. Abish has commented that "The memory of a dream to end all dreams is a vague statement. I had Hollywood in mind."[19] And the phrase, both melodramatic and euphemistic, evokes not the fact of the Holocaust, but the ways in which it has been culturally framed. It leaves the novel itself with an unresolved relation to the structure it explores, foregoing the transcendent perspective that would have allowed conclusion. The function of self-consciousness in the narrative is to ensure that its *narration* always remains integral to the argument. The emotionally charged material of the narrative is filtered through a cool, analytical narration, but the argument is not that analysis: it is the question raised by its complicity with the lure of the familiar explanation exposed by the narrative itself. What motivates this analysis? What is at stake for us? Abish situates his novel in postwar Germany finally not because that context impinges so powerfully upon the self-image of his characters, but because it does so for his readers.

Chapter 6

The Quest for Love and the Writing of Female Desire in Kathy Acker's *Don Quixote*

In general, feminist fiction has been wary of adopting innovative forms: feminist writers, like others with a polemical agenda, have tended to choose realism as the obvious mode of commitment. By contrast innovation, especially as characterized under the rubric of postmodernism, has been viewed as a frivolity. But this preference for conventional forms misses an opportunity for the expression of difference that is itself fundamental to radical feminist politics. Such a consideration has profoundly affected the more theoretically adventurous French feminist tradition—the writings of Hélène Cixous and Luce Irigaray, for example, and the project of an *écriture féminine*. In America innovative forms *have* been explored in the contexts that treat difference as an absolute, such as the separatist perspective of radical lesbianism; examples would include Joanna Russ's *The Female Man* (1975) and June Arnold's *Sister Gin* (1975). But a broad survey of the feminist attitude to innovation must conclude, as Bonnie Zimmerman does from a postmodernist perspective, that "more arguments exist for a postmodern feminist aesthetic than do examples of one."[1]

Kathy Acker, who achieved notoriety with the publication of *Blood and Guts in High School* (1984), is an exception. In *Don Quixote* she undertakes both to conduct a feminist critique of heterosexual relations and patriarchal authority, and to find a form in which female desire may be articulated and heterosexual love affirmed. *Don Quixote* engages the relation between sexuality and power, and does so obsessively, Acker's persistence contradicting the apparent nihilism of her

135

findings. It also uses radical narrative methods that locate the trauma of this confrontation in the form of the text itself. So far, so good, but this interaction of form and substance needs more careful articulation: exactly how do Acker's formal decisions in this novel contribute to its argument? To begin with, why *Don Quixote?*

Acker's *Quixote* at first sight owes little to Cervantes' original, but her own account of its inception suggests otherwise. The abortion that sets the novel in motion has an autobiographical source, and the fusion of this material with Cervantes is a result of subjective association: "Ms. Acker picked up Cervantes' text two years ago . . . when she was looking for something to divert her attention from her own impending abortion. 'I couldn't keep my mind off the abortion so I started writing down what I was reading, but the abortion kept getting into it.' "[2] This way of reading/writing closely parallels the way in which the other texts she appropriates within the novel are mutated by the preoccupations of the context into which they are imported. Such is Acker's concept of "plagiarism": she has elevated it to a formal strategy, emptied of its pejorative connotations by the blatancy of its operation. The motive is no longer to gain credit for another's work, but to access a cultural heritage too loaded with subjective significance to countenance the dissociating frame set up by attributed quotation. Her use of Cervantes, however, is at one remove, exploiting formal and thematic characteristics more often than the words themselves.

Acker's use of material and motifs from Cervantes is even more dominated by her own purposes than with her other texts, and functions really as no more than a fine thread of allusions, points of anchorage in the host text. Her Sancho Panza is not a single character but a series of largely undifferentiated dogs. The dog in Acker's work equates with Sancho Panza in that it stands in opposition to Don Quixote's madness, symbolizing deference to the imperatives of pragmatism. But pragmatism here is debased, dehumanized: it has become a crude self-interested materialism. The dogs in *Don Quixote* divide into the dehumanized victims of this ideology, those who accompany the knight at various stages through the novel; and the ideology's unabashed proponents—notably Richard Nixon and his entourage. Their doggishness manifests itself both in the debasement of their speech into barks and woofs, and in their universal designation by the ungendered pronoun "it." This is not a negation of the fact of sex, but of the human psychological dialectic between the sexes—the basis of love. So while Nixon goes home to "copulate" irredeemably with "its bitch,"[3] the neutral pronoun in the case of the dog Ville-branche who narrates A DOG'S LIFE emerges as a critical flaw in its relation to Don Quixote in the section HETEROSEXUALITY: " 'My God!' Don Quixote exclaimed. 'You're not the sexual gender I thought you were! And I love you' " (127). This ambiguity is also central to the story of Villebranche and De Franville, in which a mutual confusion of sexual identities becomes the only model for heterosexuality's salvation.

Another direct borrowing from Cervantes is the motif of the Evil Enchanters, who are identified as the enemies of free sexual and emotional expression, from Ronald Reagan to the editors of the *Times Literary Supplement* to Andrea Dworkin (101–2). The theme of enchantment is prominent in the only extended episode that closely follows Cervantes' novel, the vision of paradise (184–90) which is taken from the vision of Montesumo's Cave.[4] But Acker does not generally treat of the original *Don Quixote* in such detail; her use of Cervantes is more abstract, better seen in terms of authorial stance than textual appropriation. In fact Acker's subversive plagiarism itself allows her to claim allegiance with Cervantes on the basis of a shared concern with other texts, in Cervantes' case his parodic use of popular ballads and chivalric romances: "I write by using other written texts, rather than by expressing 'reality' which is what most novelists do. Our reality now, which occurs so much through the media, *is* other texts. I'm playing the same game as Cervantes."[5] This analogy trans-lates into thematic terms, since the chivalric code of courtly love that motivates the first Quixote finds an equivalent in Acker's novel as the obsessional romantic idea of love that possesses her knight. The transition from a courtly to a romantic concept of love, as well as from a male to a female knight, converts her protagonist's quest into a vehicle of Acker's inquiry into female sexuality and the social pressures that impinge upon it. Writing the novel in response to her reading of Cervantes, she became fascinated with the knight's "trying to transform a faintly intolerable social reality into what really is the grail, this totally romantic search. All sorts of feminist issues got involved—it just took off."[6]

The attributes Acker's Quixote derives from the original are mostly paradoxical. She adopts this identity with a self-conscious emphasis on its contradictions, deciding to "become a female-male or a night-knight" (10). Acker also plays with the tension between the old knight—her age is given as sixty-six years (18)—and her youthful (adolescent) ideal of love. But the main source of paradox is inherent in the original character himself: in both protagonists the pursuit of idealistic ends with complete disregard for pragmatic imperatives indicates an ambiguous combination of the lunatic and the visionary. THE FIRST ADVENTURE of Acker's Quixote is a paradigmatic instance of this opposition. Setting out "to right all wrongs" she intervenes in a beating with visionary fervour: "Don Quixote cried, 'Stop that! In this world which's wrong, it's wrong to beat up people younger than yourself. I'm fighting all of your culture' " (14). But her idealistic resolution of the situation displays a lunatic incomprehension of its realities:

> Don Quixote thought carefully. "You have to go back for your teacher, deep inside him, wants to help you and has just been mistaken how to help you. If he didn't care for you, he wouldn't want you back."
> The old man took the boy back to school and there flogged him even more severely. . . . The boy tried to enjoy the beating because his life couldn't be any other way. (15)

The contradictions of Acker's knight operate within a framework also appropriated from Cervantes, that of the quest. The sublime folly of this quest is established in the first paragraph, and defines the whole action of the novel: "When she was finally crazy because she was about to have an abortion, she conceived of the most insane idea that any woman can think of. Which is to love" (9). But the novel does not fulfil the expectations of a monolinear narrative aroused by this model. Acker is not concerned to produce a linear narrative because her argument does not involve the evolution of a generative scenario, but the articulation of a perspective or state of affairs. This is a shift from a representational to a discursive model of narrative, which redefines narrative coherence as the recognition of significant thematic relationships between disparate textual fragments. On this assumption, "Narrative isn't a problem anymore. Even if you use a discontinuous story people will make connections."[7] The form of Acker's work in general is not predicated upon narrative, but upon tableaux; she does not offer events but positions. Speaking of more conventional realistic narratives, she complains "when I read novels now they don't seem to have anything to do with anything. I can't tell where the writers' guts are—novels should be aimed at adding to cultural discourse."[8] There is a potential problem of momentum in such a mode of writing, its neglect of temporal development risking a disregard for the temporal activity of reading. By incorporating the narrative structure of *Don Quixote* into her novel she avoids this propensity towards aimlessness: "I won't allow myself to be cut off from the very powerful resources of the linear story. In *Don Quixote* I've laid a narrative over the cut-ups and since Cervantes' novel is episodic the problem of sequence is solved."[9] Acker's invocation of the quest, as a strongly end-directed but episodic form, is intended to achieve the maximum sense of narrative direction with the minimum commitment to narrative structure. The episodic narrative and the quest framework that unifies it operate in contradiction to each other in Acker's novel, since the sexual problematic she explores in its various scenarios does not progress, but is static, paralysed. The novel does not offer a dialectical evolution: its argument is cyclical, stalemated by a series of double-binds. The proposed structure of the quest therefore functions only potentially, as the will to escape this cycle. The cyclical nature of the narrative episodes is affirmed in the subtitle of the section THE LAST ADVENTURE, which adds UNTIL THIS BOOK WILL BEGIN AGAIN (175), as well as by the function of repetition and reiteration throughout the book, and by the series of false endings, last visions and deaths of Don Quixote. The double-bind structure of the argument is epigrammatized in several variations, of the form "If a woman insists she can and does love and her living isn't loveless or dead, she dies. So either a woman is dead or she dies" (33). This foregrounded circularity or failure to progress is modified by its tension with the form of the quest narrative. The lack of development in the narrative has less effect on the novel's momentum than the *expectation* of development that the invoked structure generates. The combination of the argument's thematic stasis with its dynamic linear structure results in the incorporation of this dynamism *within* stasis, producing an argument in dynamic equilibrium. The cyclical form that constrains the narrative is therefore not viewed from outside, as repetitious and fruitless, but from within, as a potent condition of frustration.

The dynamic equilibrium of the novel is mirrored in the arrested emotional development of its various incompletely differentiated characters. Don Quixote, Saint Simeon, Villebranche, Lulu, Juliette, and the various unnamed female narrators all share a sensibility in which obsessive sexual and emotional need is held in a constant and necessary state of frustration. Through all these characters Acker explores an emotional impasse in which the character is denied emotional freedom by the realities of her situation, but does not easily relinquish her impossible desires. As one reviewer of the novel noted, "Acker speaks from a level that is both above and below the urbanity of everyday life,"[10] in a world of fantastic desires and abject miseries which coexist but do not cancel each other. This alienation from everyday life is reflected in the dominant tone of the novel, which is both impassioned and naive, characterized by idealistic affirmations of the emotionally unattainable and declamations against the inevitable. The tone is not confined to the characters of the novel but encompasses the impersonal narration, which exhibits a close emotional affinity with the characters it narrates and tends to further merge their sensibilities. This narration appears to be at least in part directly autobiographical, functioning as a mouthpiece of the id for Acker. It also has a calculated satiric function which is most apparent in its political digressions. One early example, clearly marked off from the surrounding text as an authorial aside by the heading INSERT, begins "I think Prince should be President of the United States because all our Presidents since World War II have been stupid anyway . . ." (21). This position is defended by arguing that "Prince, unlike all our other images or fakes or Presidents, stands for values. . . . The Prince believes in feelings, fucking, and fame" (21), and is therefore both refreshingly amoralistic and (possibly) conscious.

This adamant naivety is that of adolescence, the emotional stage at which the confrontation between the self and the society to which it must accommodate is at its height; the stage in which desire and the libidinous are new and as absolute as the repressive social and political codifications that impinge upon them in every social and sexual interaction. In this way the protagonists of *Don Quixote* are all caught between a will to connect and a refusal to compromise their emotional integrity. The impossibility of social integration is assured by the antipathy of society's dominant ideals to emotional openness, its subordination of human to economic values: "Emerging militarily and economically unrivalled from the Second World War, America was uniquely and fully able to impose its hatred of nonmaterialism—its main ideal—on the remainder of the world" (72). Materialism is seen as the rational development of the drive for self-preservation, its sole value being the domination of natural, social and political structures. Hence it has become " 'the universal principle of a society which seeks to reduce all phenomena to this enlightenment ideal of rationalism, or subjugation of the other' " (72). The guardians of materialism are the evil enchanters, and Don Quixote's quest for love is therefore also a struggle against them: " 'As soon as we all stop being enchanted,' Don Quixote explained, 'Human love'll again be possible' " (102). For Don Quixote and the novel's other central characters, the alienation from the structures of authority resulting from their refusal of materialism is a state of perpetual rebellion. This estrangement from social values is extreme; Acker's characters are absolutely unreconciled, in a way that would be impossible to sustain against the forces of social reality. Their continuous hovering on the brink of emotional self-destruction is, within the context of the novel (subtitled "which was a dream") a nightmare condition of arrested or cyclical time. This dream sense is accentuated by the repetition and variation of its essential narrative and the sense of entrapment generated by the novel's false development. Its function for the reader is analogous to the access to the unconscious a dream can provide, exposing lost or suppressed selves that have been obscured by the framework of assimilation to a socialized condition, the assimilation Acker's characters refuse.

The *strangeness* of the world of *Don Quixote* provides opportunity for the reader to acknowledge the price of socialization. By elevating

absolute loyalty to primal emotions from a presocial stage of development into a state of being, the novel defamiliarizes these emotions
and exposes them to the reader's own self-consciousness. The access
it offers to the reader's impossible lost selves is one of the novel's
most considerable affective strengths. By engaging with social reality
in ways that reality does not allow, but which are discernibly present
in the mentality individuals relinquish in the process of assimilation,
Acker calls into question the values prioritized by society and by our
construction of it. It is a function that also operates in Acker's other
work—the primacy of the naive, the adolescent, and the presocial is
even present in several of her books' titles: *The Childlike Life of the
Black Tarantula*; *Blood and Guts in High School*; and, by invoking the
Bildungsroman genre, *Great Expectations*. Acker's comments on art
and her own writing also support the argument for this orientation's
centrality to her concept of *Don Quixote* and the novels that preceded
it. She affirms her allegiance to a sensibility unreconciled to society,
emphasizing and privileging inarticulateness, a concept of art as prerational expression, as the direct articulation of inner emotions unmediated by logical or aesthetic consideration for the culture to which it
addresses itself. She wishes to resist mimesis in favour of an expressive
function for art, and seeks to subvert the concept of description by
characterizing it as a belated imposition upon the reality it purports
to represent: "The act of describing assumes one event can be a
different event: meaning dominates or controls existence. But desire—or art—is."[11] The direct equation of desire and art identifies the
concerns of the latter as exactly the prerational libidinous realm that
is evoked in *Don Quixote*. It also insists upon the asocial quality of
artistic production, denying it any formative intent or design upon its
audience, either aesthetic or didactic. But this refusal of any purpose-
ful address in art is not intended to deny it any cultural value. In fact
it is exactly the insubordinate self-presentation of art, as a refusal to
submit to the parameters of the ruling culture by which it is framed
and homogenized, that constitutes its value. Acker wants art to confront the culture to which it presents itself *unframed*, rather than
already contained by a process of self-description or self-distancing,
which she sees as a form of pre-emptive criticism:

If art's to be more than craft, more than decorations for the people in power, it's this want, this existence. . . . Examine the two statements, "Help!" and "I need help." The first language is a cry; the second, a description. Only the cry, art, rather than the description or criticism, is primary. The cry is stupid, it has no mirror; it communicates.

I want to cry.[12]

This concept of art as a cry insists that it does not offer itself as a self-sufficient reflection of the artist's engagement with reality, but as a raw artistic enactment of it, the value of which is determined by the way its readers or audience are able to confront and respond to it. The definition is appropriate to the argument of *Don Quixote,* and is supported by the literary practice of the knight herself: " 'I wasn't sent to Oxford or anywhere, so what I do to write is cut crosses into the insides of my wrists. I write in fever' " (107).

Acker's novel deals very directly with the expression of desire and the confrontation of limitations imposed upon its expression and fulfilment. These limitations include those of political, moral and religious origin as well as the hazards of sexual politics. The central issue is always a confrontation between desire and control, between immediacy and structural imposition. In political terms Acker's advocacy of desire translates into a pursuit of individual freedom, an anarchic response to authority. In America, Land of Freedom, this involves an exposure of those establishment myths of freedom which consolidate the power structure. Acker's view of American society is Hobbesian, her canine vision of humanity a metaphor of the materialist reduction of society, and therefore human relations, to Hobbes' state of nature: " 'Doggish life depends upon unequal power relations or the struggle of power. This is the society in which we live. The life of a dog, even if the dog's dead like me, is solitary, poor, nasty, brutish, short. The condition of a dog is a condition of war, of everyone against everyone: so every dog has a right to everything, even to another dog's body. This is freedom' " (114). Acker offers a series of demystifications of America's myths of freedom. These take the form of possible answers to the question "What are the myths of the beginning of America?" (117) followed by explanations justifying their formulation, which in each case is sub-versively paradoxical:

> Answer: The desire for religious intolerance made America or Freedom.

> Explanation: . . . these New Worlders had left England not because they had been forbidden there to worship as they wanted to but be-cause there they and, more important, their neighbors weren't forced to live as rigidly in religious terms as they wanted. (117–18)

There emerges from this reading of the founding myths of America an equation between Puritans and politicians, Quakers and citizens, which leaves no place in the system between political authoritarian-ism and pacifistic abdication from control: "Answer: Individual free-dom was the choice between militarism and the refusal to partake in government" (119). Acker's protagonists defy this absence of political freedom by their alienation from the system, which is a refusal of its parameters. Don Quixote writes for and of the outcast, among whom she includes all women who refuse "the bickerings and constraints of heterosexual marriage" (202). But she insists that they exist in a condition of deprivation, not an alternative community: " 'The only characteristic freaks share is our knowledge that we don't fit in. Anywhere. It is for you, freaks my loves, I am writing and it is about you' " (202). Acker's own concentration upon the outcast, "freaks," derives theoretical support from Julia Kristeva's concept of "abjec-tion" which relates the formation of structures in society to the process of exclusion by which it operates, and identifies a subversive potential in "defilement," embracing this exclusion as a positive value. Acker's protagonists are abjects not only in relation to the dominant social structures but also in relation to themselves, to the form of a stable ego which constitutes an established position vis-à-vis society. So Lulu, in Acker's plagiarism of Wedekind's *Earth-Spirit* and *Pandora's Box,* can defy Schön: "You can't change me cause there's nothing to change. I've never been" (78). For Kristeva it is exactly this quality of abjection that demonstrates the constitutive function of absence in differential structures including, with particular significance for Acker, the structure of desire: "There is nothing like the abjection of self to show that all abjection is in fact recognition of the *want* on which any being, meaning, language or desire is founded."[13] The primacy of desire for Acker's characters is therefore also the guarantee of their suffering and their failure. The affirmation of desire is necessarily an introduction of absence into the self.

At the beginning of the novel Don Quixote meets a young Irish Catholic who has come to London and lost her possessions in the process of concealing her abortion from her friends and family. The confrontation with Catholicism enlarges into a more general antagonism between religion and the autonomy of individual desires that culminates in Don Quixote's "Battle Against the Religious White Men" in which she proposes to lead the pack of dogs " 'in a fight to death or to life against the religious white men and against all the alienation that their religious image-making or control brings to humans' " (178). This confrontation is worked out largely in the contested religious imagery of blood and virginity that punctuates the novel. Don Quixote's quest is framed by blood from her abortion to her defeat and death, as her final will to the dogs records: " 'Dogs of this world. You are holding bleeding flesh between your sharp reddened teeth. I recognize this flesh because it's mine' " (201). The knight suffers as a parodic female Christ-figure. But whereas the alienated wild dogs flock around her, "Probably because they smelt she was about to get her period" (177), to men " ' "nuclear bomb leakage's less dangerous than ours" ' " (173). The antithesis of blood is virginity, a condition of denial which is presented as the universal sexual character of women: " 'Women are bitches, dog. They're the cause of the troubles between men and women. Why? Because they don't give anything, they deny. Female sexuality has always been denial or virginity' " (27). But this sexuality has been defined by male religion, and is both the cause and result of misogyny: " 'Religious white men hate women because and so they make women into the image of the Virgin Mary' " (178). Affirmation of blood over virginity is therefore a subversion of women's socialized sexual role and a refusal of the prescriptions of religion. It is also opening up to desire, and so to suffering: " ' "I'll whip you by breaking you down by breaking through your virginity or identity. As soon as you're no

longer a virgin, you're going to leak. You'll keep on leaking so you
won't be able to retain any more of their teachings. . . . I have to
warn you. As soon as you start leaking, you're going to need desperately. You won't be secure ever again" ' " (173).

The forces opposing the free expression of desire are similarly
manifest in the repressive code of social morality and the internalizing
of this code in the process of social integration. The novel presents a
vision of socialization according to Hobbes, who ironically proposes
hope and good actions as the pleasures of his "canine" society.
Returned to haunt Nixon as the Angel of Death, he relentlessly
makes explicit the meaning of his teachings: " 'What is this hope and
good actions? . . . I think either by receiving thoughts or by wanting.
Wanting's either thoughtless or, being taught, resembles receiving. In
short, I'm a dog. My hope and actions're mechanical' " (113). The
family as a mode of social integration is also confronted in the novel.
In "A Portrait of an American Family," the prodigal daughter returns
from the horrors of New York to the safety of her family. Her
reception is presented as a rapid transformation of the environment
of love and security for which she returned into a nightmare of
constraint: "You were perfectly right to come back here. . . . The
family is the only refuge any of us has. Daddy and I've been discussing
this. . . . It's normal for children to break from their parents. You
wanted to wallow in the outside world. You wallowed in all the
hatred and filth that is outside. . . . You've come back to prison of
your own free accord. . . . From now on, you will do whatever I
woof you to do and, more important, be whoever I order you. This
is a safe unit" (116). The scene ends in a total annihilation of self as
the father has his daughter electrocuted while watching on television.
Against the repressions of social respectability Acker uses pornography, as a total embrace of unregulated desire which works both to
confront the reader's taboos and to liberate and lay bare the sexuality
of the participating characters. This exploration of sexuality is never
sanitized, and includes an extended plagiarism of Sade—the tension
between sexual freedom and sexual degradation is not ignored but
heightened, as a means of exposing the raw nerves of sexual relations.
In the episode from Sade's *Juliette*, Juliette's violent sexual education
is given traumatic form by the triple and quadruple repetition of

each paragraph of its progress. But the trauma does lead to sexual enlightenment: when Juliette is able to articulate the contradictions of her sexuality and social identity, the repetitions cease.

The primary oppressive power relationship in the novel is that between the sexes: the quest for love that motivates Don Quixote and her surrogates is impeded less by the external forces of society than by the structure of sexual relations themselves. This denies mutuality in love because it is a structure of domination in which the controlling (male) sex defines the other as object in the mechanism of desire. Reciprocal love is frustrated by desire's objectifying function: " ' "When you love us, you hate us because we have to deny you. Why? Objects can't love back" ' " (28). Since the sexual dominance that orientates the objectification of desire is socially encoded, the sexuality of the oppressed sex is already negated and her desire within the social framework of sexuality is pre-empted. To speak the language of desire involves adopting a subject position that the oppressed sex is denied by the grammar of that language: " ' "I'm your desire's object, dog, because I can't be the subject. Because I can't be a subject: what you name 'love,' I name 'nothingness.' I won't not be: I'll perceive and I'll speak" ' " (28). Acker's portrayal of women as occluded in sexual relations owes much to Luce Irigaray.[14] Irigaray's analysis of the concept of woman defined by men as an absence or void—and of the commodification of women as sexual goods—is present in all the book's sexual relations, but most concisely in Acker's insertion of Wedekind's Lulu into the plot of Shaw's *Pygmalion*. In the first section of this text, "The Selling of Lulu," Lulu's father Schigold sells her to Schön: "The girl belongs to me. You got her. Don't you believe in free enterprise?" (79). And when Schön, whose "social experiment" is to make Lulu into something out of nothing, finally reacts against the paternal/sexual relationship he has evolved with her, he is recoiling from the threat posed by the absence he has defined: "I hate you, hole. . . . I will not have you show me love. You are nothing, nothing. I will not have you break into my world, break me up, destroy me" (89–90).

For Acker the central issue of feminism is the need to affirm female sexuality without accepting the social determination this sexuality implies in a male-dominated society. She formulates it as the fundamental paradox of feminist dissent: "On the left, and on the right, and in the middle and everywhere, men have used women's sexualities and sexual needs and desires in order to control women. . . . One result of this historical situation is that heterosexual women find themselves in a double-bind: If they want to fight sexism, they must deny their own sexualities. At the same time, feminism cannot be about the denial of any female sexuality."[15] Acker's feminism is not a definitive condemnation of sexual relations, but always seeking to recuperate some viable form for them. She repudiates the separatist tendency in feminism, preferring the dangerous quest for a liberated heterosexuality. As a result her characters are vulnerable and desperate: they have no autonomy but are almost wholly other-directed. As Cindy Patton observes, "The voice of her women is much more ambiguous than the idealized 'strong woman' of much feminist fiction."[16] *Don Quixote* includes its own parable of this dissent from hard political commitment in order to acknowledge individual susceptibility to painful desire. Don Quixote has three friends, the Leftist, the Liberal and the feminist:

> Don Quixote's friends dragged her toward her bed, which was a mattress on the floor, but just as they were dragging her across the floor, they saw she didn't have any wounds. They didn't need to care for or love her.
> "My wound is inside me. It is the wound of lack of love. . . ."
> Her friends, aghast at femininity, determined to burn it out. (16–17)

But Acker's stance is not apolitical; it rather detects in affirmative autobiographical feminist fiction a complicity with the ground rules of contemporary political control that she wishes to subvert:

> For some feminists the autobiographical mode is the form of political defiance. Well, there are many levels of coming out of oppression and it was important at one stage to say "Me," and to ask "Who am I?" But that strategy simply doesn't interest me. Writing which says all the time "here I am, and I want, I want . . ." presents a Hobbist universe which suits Reagan and Thatcher fine. Autobiography really is selfish.[17]

Acker is concerned to affirm the possibility of an I/other relationship, to acknowledge desire at the price of emotional vulnerability. For her, sexual emancipation cannot wait upon political emancipation. "The connecting thread in Acker's work is her insistence on expressing sexual desire now, even before we have created a safer world for those desires to find their practice."[18] In *Don Quixote* the knight affirms early on her need to connect, and all subsequent impediments are related to the conditions for this realization of desire, which are the reciprocal identity of love's object and its subject, and the unity of the sexual and the emotional:

> "Why can't I just love?"
> "Because every verb to be realized needs its object. Otherwise, having nothing to see, it can't see itself or be. Since love is sympathy or communication, I need an object which is both subject and object: to love, I must love a soul. Can a soul exist without a body? Is physical separate from mental? Just as love's object is the appearance of love; so the physical realm is the appearance of the godly: the mind is the body. This," she thought, "is why I've got a body." (10)

As the inadequacy of conventional sexual relations to these criteria is amply demonstrated, Acker considers a series of alternatives: the will in the novel to establish sexual relations in a form that involves no self-negation or subjugation leads along convoluted paths of sexual inversion and sado-masochistic experimentation. The strategies against the dominant sexual power relations that are explored— gender confusion, sexual deviancy, lesbianism—are all ultimately failures; their attacks on the power structure of sexual relations are misdirected, working not to rectify this structure but to avoid, ignore or invert it.

Villebranche resolves to have nothing to do with men, seeking refuge in lesbianism: " 'Since women when they make love to each other're both controlling, there's no question of control or power between them' " (127). This is unsatisfactory because her lesbianism is not a fulfilment of desire but an avoidance of it, as she is not attracted to women: " 'Since I didn't want to sleep with women, sleeping with women couldn't endanger me, didn't touch the ranting, raving unknown. A woman, rather than being the unknown, is my mirror' " (126–7). She turns instead to the androgynous De Franville, bidding for control of the relationship by wooing him as a Nazi captain. This mutual gender confusion—they are referred to throughout as "she(he)" and "he(she)" respectively—evolves into a stalemate of erotic unattainability. In an attempt to break the deadlock, they reconcile themselves to being controlled by adopting sadomasochistic roles: " 'How could I eradicate, not my being controlled, but my fear of being controlled? By being controlled as much as possible' " (134). As their educational sado-masochism reaches extremes, the sexual ambiguity is lost, and with it the balance of controlling and being controlled. The transition is marked by a change to the unambiguous third person pronoun:

> "Due to my increased ferocity, she(he) twists so much that for the first time just as my whip strokes have become hard enough to make her(him) realize that the pain isn't pretense that pain is only pain and eradicates all pretense and stupid thinking, she(he) reveals a fault that is absolute. She(He) had actually tricked me.
> "Then, I hit him without control. I hit him cause I hated him."
> (139–40)

Through pain they grow from a fear of the functions of domination and submission implied by their sexuality to an acceptance of it: " 'This man had no intention of taking responsibility, for he hated and feared his masculinity as much as I did. By making all this pain clear, both he and I for the first time accepted that sex' " (140). They have not changed the parameters of their sexuality, but wilfully submitted themselves to it by embracing a regime of violence and pain: "Don Quixote was disgusted that human heterosexuality had come to such an extreme end" (141).

The section AN EXAMINATION OF WHAT KIND OF SCHOOLING WOMEN NEED plagiarizes Sade's *Juliette* in order to explore the emotional possibilities of a sexual world entirely outside "healthy" society: " 'Living here in disease and being diseased strangely bring us closer to each other: we can now have emotions for each other. We don't care about the people who control us. . . . the world of almost total death's the world of almost freedom. The closer we're living to total human death, the weaker the socio-political constraints on us' " (104). Acker excludes all of Sade's male characters to develop the sexual power play between women. First, the acknowledgement of sexual pleasure and pain forces Juliette out of her socially defined passivity or nonexistence: " ' "My physical sensations scare me because they confront me with a self when I have no self: sexual touching makes these physical sensations so fierce, I'm forced to find a self when I've been trained to be nothing" ' " (171). This physical enlightenment is pursued to the extremes of pain, and the assertion of sexual identity to the extremes of subjugation of the other, until Juliette takes on the vestments of a man: " 'Unfortunately I didn't know how to fuck Laure. Desperately I strapped a dildo around my waist. I was aghast: wearing a dildo is like wearing plastic. Is wearing plastic. I was no longer natural' " (174). She takes Laure's virginity in panic, but emotionally refuses the role she is enacting: " 'I made Laure wail. . . . I was more terrified by what I was doing now than I had been by my strapping on the dildo. How could I be doing this to one whom I loved? I wailed as loudly as the child' " (175). The women succeed only in recreating the abuses of male sexual dominance, albeit with painful self-awareness.

The novel does not affirm any possibility for equal sexual relations, but neither does it confirm the absence of any possibility. The attempted relations it explores all end in failure, but without extinguishing the want that motivated them. It does allow a solipsistic interpretation of its failure to establish a viable form for love or the relationship of self to other:

> A real vision: There's no longer nature: trees bushes, mainly: unboxed space and time. There're only rooms. Whatever you do, whether you're successful or unsuccessful, you are only in some room.
> The vision is: there's no joy. (190)

But the novel's ending is a (limited) refutation of this nihilistic vision. Don Quixote has a dream in which she accepts the impossibility of relations with men, or her "master." She turns away from the self-negation imposed upon her by her master's sexuality, equating its absolute power with the power of God, until God intervenes:

> "Suddenly, I heard my master's voice. 'Shut up.
> " 'Where, where in hell—from Hell?—did you get your idea that I am male?' " (206)

He proceeds to discredit his identity with absolute manhood by relating the verdict of Satan: " ' "he has no respect for me because I make love to old women, spinster virgins. That he personally would rather boil over in a fourteen-year-old cunt, even if it is rape, than hide beneath his mother's skirts. He's a real man whereas I'm a mealy-mouth hypocrite, dishonest" ' " (207). If God is inadequate to Satan's standards of manhood the concept of male sexuality as an absolute, fixed in the transcendent order of things, is specious. The Absolute is self-discredited, of indeterminate gender, and unavailable as the rationale of a predetermined structure for sexual relations: " 'God continued condemning Him- or Herself: "So now that you know I'm imperfect, night, that you can't turn to Me: turn to yourself" ' " (207). It is no longer possible for Don Quixote to lay the failure of her sexuality at the door of an absolute male sexual code. The knight accepts these teachings and ascends from her dream to re-engage the world: " 'As I walked along beside Rocinante, I thought about God for one more minute and forgot it. I closed my eyes, head drooping, like a person drunk for so long she no longer knows she's drunk, and then, drunk, awoke to the world which lay before me' " (207). It is a qualified affirmation, suggesting no resolution, no success but the survival of the will. The cycle of defeats inflicted upon Don Quixote's quest for love leaves behind a residue of desire. This remnant, which is the continuing will to connect, to find a viable form of love, is Acker's primary value and her refutation of emotional nihilism.

Don Quixote's quest is not resolved or abandoned, but reaffirmed in the last of the novel's cycles, the cycle of day and night, which identifies the quest with existence itself. This cyclical form, which is essential to the novel's argument, also has a strategic function. Acker's use of this reiterative, episodic narrative model allows her to intro-

duce multiple subnarratives; the continuity of the text being a function of thematic characteristics and the quest framework she takes
from Cervantes, its substance has the freedom of extreme discontinuity. The function of this discontinuity is to create a plurality of textual
articulations and so subvert any monolithic narratorial identity. This
is again related to the theories of Luce Irigaray, to her equation of
women's sexuality and hence women's writing with multiplicity,
with the absence of a single voice: "Her sexuality, always at least
double, goes even further: it is *plural*. Is this the way culture is seeking
to characterize itself now? Is this the way texts write themselves/
are written now? Without quite knowing what censorship they are
evading?"[19] The plurality of Acker's texts is quite self-conscious, her
use of plagiarism being a strategy central to this process, as she
explains in interview: "I've always seen writing as to do with attacking the ego, breaking down the autobiographical 'I,' playing a
range of voices against each other in the text. That's a golden light I
see in Dickens, that plurality of voices, and that's why, until very
recently, I've worked by juxtaposing other people's texts, representing our cultural inheritance, attacking any central, moral voice. So
plagiarism became a strategy of originality."[20] Plagiarism, then, is
both an attack on the autobiographical "I" and a strategy of originality: not an abdication of authorial control, but a textualization of it.
Acker uses it throughout *Don Quixote,* but most explicitly in part
two, "Other Texts," which is her most extreme abuse of the novel's
narrative framework, justified by a cursory subheading: BEING
DEAD, DON QUIXOTE COULD NO LONGER SPEAK. BEING
BORN INTO AND PART OF A MALE WORLD, SHE HAD NO
SPEECH OF HER OWN. ALL SHE COULD DO WAS READ MALE
TEXTS WHICH WEREN'T HERS (39). This section of the novel
bases itself upon four texts: Bely's *Petersburg,* Lampedusa's *The Leopard,* the Japanese monster movie *Godzilla versus Megalon* and Wedekind's *Earth-spirit* and *Pandora's Box.* According to Tom LeClair the
point is that "Quixote has to read works by four male writers who
create or unwillingly perpetuate harmful stereotypes of women"
which "Ms. Acker bashes with broad parody and grotesque revision."[21] This is to mistake the purpose of Acker's revisionary plagiarism, which is not polemical but expressive. It does not engage the

original texts directly or coherently enough to constitute a critique of
their perpetuation of "harmful stereotypes of women," which is in
any case not a quality they all obviously share; it is rather a process by
which these texts are bent to the purposes of her own thematic
concerns. For while her use of plagiarism is a foregrounding of
textuality over authorial identity, an insistence upon the primacy of
given language over the mythic process of creative origination, it is
not a denial of the authorial role per se. If so, David Van Leer's
objection to the use of plagiarism and discontinuity would certainly
be pertinent: "Fragmenting or plagiarizing the narrative voice does
not 'deconstruct' the self. It only refocusses attention where Acker
least wishes it—back on the author."[22] Acker's plagiarism *does* return
the reader to the plagiarizing author, because it is not an attempt to
hide behind other texts, but to appropriate them. Her plagiarism is
not a mechanical principle but a highly subjective revisionary process,
in which the plagiarized text is overwhelmed by the preoccupations
she imposes upon it. This is clearly evident in her use of a poem by
Catullus ("Miser Catulle, desinas ineptire . . .") which is surrounded
by a highly idiosyncratic gloss and critical analysis. The Latin text
itself is printed with interjections that enact the erratic subjective
process of its reading:

> Nunc iam illa non vult: tu quoque,
>   impotens can't fuck any
>   boyfriends these days, bad
>   mood no wonder I'm acting
>   badly, noli NO
> nec quae fugit sectare, nec miser
>   vive
> good advice sed obstinata mente
>   perfer, obdura.
> vale, puella. (my awful telephone
>   call . . .) (48)

More explicitly, her use of Lampedusa's *The Leopard* includes a direct
statement of its subjective significance:

> The world is memory. I don't remember anymore because I refuse
> to remember anymore because all my memories hurt.

The Leopard equals these memories. I'll remember: I won't repress I won't be a zombie, despite the pain, I will have life. This's why *The Leopard's* romantic. (63)

This self-assertive plagiarism, like the reading of *Don Quixote* that Acker records as the origin of her novel, implies a close association between her mode of writing and a mode of reading: reading not as the reception of a text, but as an interaction between an active, subjective reader and a text always regarded as open or underdetermined. This is also the mode of reading that her work invites. In a review of *Empire of the Senseless,* Danny Karlin has objected that "The shock-value of such writing is diffused by the context of its literary production; readers who buy this book have already read it." Certainly shock-value is by now a derelict literary attribute: but this is only an objection if it is assumed that Acker really intends to subject the reader to " 'ultimate outrage' . . . [the] commodity being peddled by her agents and publishers. . . ."[23] The only readers she is likely to shock are those such publicity is sure to deter. Those who persevere in spite of the dust jacket are looking for, and find, something rather different—a novel that, rather than reaching out to seize the reader, presents itself as an alien but potentially recognizable textual other with which the reader may engage.

Writing and reading are equated as forms of an interface between self and text. This coexistence of textuality and subjectivity is enacted in some of the novel's stylistic mannerisms, which tend to combine rigid textual formalism with extreme idiosyncrasy. Acker's embedded narratives call for frequent doubling and tripling of quotation marks, which is done faithfully and reiterated with each new paragraph according to convention, even where this continues over many pages and a great diversity of material. (There are exceptions, such as the slippage of quotation marks by which Villebranche's consciousness is made to merge with that of Sade's Juliette in the section "Reading: I Dream my Schooling"). But this regard for the mechanics of the text is extended to Acker's frequent use of brackets, which are similarly doubled up when embedded, and reopened without having closed when beginning a new paragraph; also her use of the colon to indicate speech in dramatic form, which is reiterated with each new paragraph. This extension of the conventions applying to quotation marks presents itself as extreme deference to textual form, but its effect is defiantly individualistic.

The same sort of effect is achieved on a semantic level by Acker's use of "or" to link two equivalents rather than alternatives. This device (with its variants "which is," "that is") is ubiquitous in the novel, and creates the impression of a philosophical discourse in which the argument proceeds by establishing the logical equivalence of certain central concepts. In fact the connection between concepts that are related in this manner is rarely one of necessary equivalence, but is highly associative. Concepts are yoked not on the basis of any general logical identity but according to their previous connection in a specific, often emotionally charged context. Aside from its significant fusion of the subjective and the objective, this raising of affective association to the level of logical equivalence contributes significantly to the atmosphere of the novel. The dominant motifs expressing the themes of the impossibility of sexual relations, the negation of woman, the constriction of social and political conditions and the perverse persistence of desire all become so inextricably intertwined that the sense of imprisonment within a matrix of contradictory imperatives is tangible in the writing.

Another stylistic choice that enacts the coexistence of the personal and textual is Acker's persistent abbreviation of all parts of the verb *to be,* not just in speech but also in narrative report. The obvious effect of such a mannerism is to suggest the idiom of speech, creating a strong sense of a narrating individual, of the text as transcribed speech. But Acker's use of it extends so far beyond normal speech idiom as to actually reverse that tendency, presenting instead a defamiliarizing textual device: " 'That's how males're' " (148). This negation of the idiomatic character of the device is supported by an actual discussion of the verb within the text which suggests its implication in an obtrusive metaphysic. The context is the exegesis of Catullus, a meditation on separation and the tyranny of time:

The first main verb is *is,* an *is* which isn't Platonic. This common *is* leads to the first person subjunctives, *fear* and *hinder,* as well as

the *is'* subject noun, *fear.* This kind of time or the world makes
human fear.

Common time's other or enemy is death. *Is* is bounded by
death. So the other of *is* is *be without* in the present tense. (50)

Being in time is infected with its other by the condition of being
without. Being is attenuated by separation, so the state of separation
or lack of connection that dominates the novel is reflected in its
attenuation of all forms of *to be.*

Acker's narrative disruption, then, does not destroy the sense of
authorial identity, but ultimately turns the reader's attention back
upon it, as the orchestrator of the disruptions. This is true to some
extent in the autobiographical sense, as in the abortion on which *Don
Quixote* is founded. There is a core autobiographical narrative that
runs through all of Acker's novels, the salient features of which are
neatly summarized in *Don Quixote,* though by Villebranche rather
than the impersonal narrator:

> "These are the particulars of my life: when I was a puppy, I lived
> among rich dogs because my family was haute bourgeoisie; I was a
> special mutt in dog society because I was trained to think that way.
> I lived on the outskirts of, in the lowest part of, society because I
> worked a sex show; then I believed that I deserved to be shat on,
> that if I didn't pull myself up by my nonexistent bootstraps out of
> the muck I would die, and that I had to be very tough. I was a
> member of a certain group—the art world—whose members,
> believing that they're simultaneously society's outcasts and its
> myths, blow up their individual psychologies into general truths.
> Do these three canine identities have anything to do with each
> other?" (112)

Even here the authorial self is presented as a plurality of selves,
personae seeking rather than signifying identity. Similarly the subjectivity of her use of plagiarism means the reader's attention is returned
to the author, but it is a return to the author-as-reader, now implicated in language rather than generating it. This is the subject of
a self-referential element to the novel's argument—its ambivalent
consideration of language as a structure of communication to which

the individual must subordinate her or himself. This ambivalence originates in the difficulties of the self-other relationship that preoccupy Acker, the conflict between woman's desire to connect and her fear of subjugating the self. The position of woman is characterized throughout both as a subjugation to language and as a disinheritance from it. Men have attempted to exercise control, " 'first, by changing women; second, when this didn't work because women are stubborn creatures, by simply lying, by saying that women live only for men's love. An alteration of language, rather than of material, usually changes material conditions . . . ' " (27). An instance of this control is the power to name, an aspect of the experience of Acker's Lulu that is present in both Wedekind and, in the larger context of the power of language, *Pygmalion*. Schön's command of language is the instrument by which Lulu is stripped of identity:

> Lulu: I don't know *what* you are.
> Schön: *Who* I am.
> Lulu: Who I am.
> Schön: You do not know who you are because you do not know how to speak properly. (78)

And Schigold consolidates his mercantile rights as her father by asserting his power to name and unname:

> Schigold: . . . What's a fifty to you? What's Lulu to me?
> Schön: Lulu? Is that her name?
> Schigold: Of course not. What's in a name? (80)

Therefore the knight, as she faces her abortion at the beginning of the novel, has to name herself. Acker plays with her own name, punning upon "hack" and "hackneyed," and the instrument of abortion, the catheter: "So, she decided, 'catheter' is the glorification of 'Kathy.' By taking on such a name which, being long, is male, she would be able to become a female-male or a night-knight" (10). The quest for love is all along tied up with the problem of finding a position from which woman can speak. But the nonconformism of the quest denies the possibility of community upon which communication depends, as Don Quixote discovers: " 'TO MYSELF: I was wrong to be right, to write, to be a knight, to try to do anything:

because having a fantasy's just living inside your own head. Being a fanatic separates you from other people. If you're like everyone else, you believe opinions or what you're told. What else is there? Oh nothingness, I have to have visions, I can't have visions, I have to love: I have to be wrong to write' " (36).

As with the knight so with Lulu, the alternative to accepting the norms of society by which the community of language is established is to lapse into autism:

> Schön: . . . I have nothing more to say to you because you will not be worth speaking to until you learn to be a person and to act in manners acceptable to this society.
>
> (Lulu looks around her and no longer bothers to speak to anyone because IT ISN'T WORTH COMMUNICATING ANY MORE.) (83)

Alienation from society is alienation from speech. For woman, this means communication is incompatible with her sexuality. At the end of the Sade episode, when Juliette's attempts at masculine mastery of Laure have ended with both women wailing in pain and fear, language and sexuality come together:

> "Delbène: 'Shut the fuck up. What are you: women? Do women always wail? . . . Do women take no responsibility for their own actions and therefore have no speech of their own, no real or meaningful speech?'
>
> " 'No,' I managed to reply. 'I'm coming.' Those were my words." (175)

Juliette can have no language but the affirmation of her sexuality. Whether this language can have meaning depends upon the possibility of it finding or establishing community. The knight in her madness offers two conflicting visions of the possibility of attaining a meaningful language outside the dominant discourse. The first is optimistic: " 'I write words whom I don't and can't know, to you who will always be other than and alien to me. These words sit on the edges of meanings and aren't properly grammatical. For where there is no country, no community, the speaker's unsure of which language to use, how to speak, if it's possible to speak. Language is community. Dogs, I'm now inventing a community for you and me' " (191). Here community is the creation of language. Later the reverse possibility is faced: " 'I wanted to find a meaning or myth or language that was mine, rather than those which try to control me; but language is communal and here is no community' " (194–5). The novel does not provide a resolution, nor does Acker believe there is one, but commits herself to using the language that defines her in a way that can communicate its rebellion only in its inarticulateness: "I write. I want to write I want my writing to be meaningless I want my writing to be stupid. But the language I use isn't what I want and make, it's what's given to me. Language is always a community. Language is what I know and is my cry."[24]

Conclusion

I have dealt at length with a few important novels because it seemed the best way to give a detailed account of the often subtle qualities of their innovation, without representing this as the limit of their significance. To have attempted a general survey would have been to risk a superficial preoccupation with the *fact* of innovation, at the expense of a clear recognition of its specific literary functions. Such an approach would merely repeat the critical distortions to which innovative fiction has been subjected, and which I have sought to correct. But although the five novels I have examined here cannot adequately represent the wealth of significant innovative fiction that has been produced by American writers since the sixties, they do demonstrate some of the vitality and range of that fiction. Barthelme, in *The Dead Father,* presents a multifaceted metaphor of relations of power by combining the solidity of dialogue with the imagination of fable. In this way his measured, witty consideration of the problems of succession and the prospects for ameliorating those power relations achieves a cumulative affective resonance. By contrast, Reed's *Flight to Canada* engages with African-American history in the broad gestures of an almost cartoon satire in order to elaborate his concept of cultural slavery. The protean energy of this defiantly anachronistic and syncretic narrative succeeds in making his HooDoo aesthetic both articulation and affirmation of the politics of multiculturalism. Coover's carnivalesque fantasy in *The Public Burning* shares this comic exuberance, yet anchors it in a meticulous documentation of the politics and society of the McCarthy era. He makes the Rosenberg

161

executions exemplify the violence of America's adherence to the
ruling narratives of the Cold War, and uses his own narrative to
inscribe and implicate the reader in the process. Abish, too, is concerned with the individual's investment in national identity, but
addresses a situation in which the fragility and incoherence of such
structures provokes a crisis of self-conscious analysis. In *How German
Is It* the social fabric of the postwar "New Germany" is torn apart by
the return of the repressed past; but this defamiliarization is made to
operate both inside and outside the narrative frame, so that the
novel's analytic detachment is ultimately exposed as a subterfuge and
our investment in this explanatory structure itself is brought into
question. Acker's *Don Quixote* is concerned less with the self than
with the possibility of relation, pursuing an impossible quest for love
innocent of the sexual politics of patriarchal culture. By means of
radical strategies of plagiarism, pornography and alienation from language itself, the novel communicates the force of a desire that it
simultaneously represents as strictly asocial and inarticulate.

This body of fiction is impressive not only in the scope of its
engagement with significant concerns (both perennial and contemporary), but also in the imaginative resourcefulness it brings to those
concerns. The formal inventiveness of innovative fiction implies a
belief in the ultimate seriousness of imagination; it is a recognition of
the potential for discovery that can be released by a more expansive
concept of the nature of fiction. Indeed, nowhere is the breadth of
fictional imagination displayed to better effect than in the innovative
writing of recent American novelists. The five writers I have discussed have themselves produced a wealth of fiction beyond the few
works treated here, and the list of other names I might rehearse is
extensive. From the narrative garrulousness of John Barth or Raymond Federman to the fragmentary lyricism of Richard Brautigan,
Guy Davenport or Clarence Major; from the encyclopedic prodigal-
ity of Thomas Pynchon, William Gaddis or Joseph McElroy to the
cool irony of Max Apple, Harold Jaffe or Leonard Michaels; from the
apocalyptic intensity of William Burroughs to the warm satire of Kurt
Vonnegut, Joanna Russ or Jonathan Baumbach; the verbal sensuality
of William Gass or Gilbert Sorrentino to the jazzy improvisations of

Ronald Sukenick or Steve Katz—the imaginative life of this fiction is as unbounded as any to which the contemporary reader might turn. More fundamentally, the work of these writers has changed the ground rules of fiction for others. Without their example, it would be difficult to conceive of the very effective blends of realistic and fabulistic narrative in Tim O'Brien's *Going After Cacciato* or Toni Morrison's *Beloved*, or E. L. Doctorow's ironic manipulations of history in *Ragtime* and *Loon Lake*, or the narrative reflexiveness of Don DeLillo's *Ratner's Star*.

Innovative writing, by exceeding the formal limits of mimesis, has greatly enhanced the imaginative possibilities of the novel. But when fictions of this sort began to appear in increasing numbers in the sixties, the critical concept of fiction was largely defined in terms of mimetic representation: under those circumstances, such formal freedom could only be conceived of as the novel's antithesis, if not its nemesis. Accordingly, the critical attention to this fiction became preoccupied with formal innovation in its own right. Such formal features as the playfulness of its narrative, its fictional self-consciousness and its linguistic immanence were seized upon as ends rather than means, and so became indicators of the autonomy of innovative fiction. Once the critical agenda had been set, it seemed that both the advocates and the critics of innovative fiction could do little but declare themselves by their response to that fiction's supposed autonomy. Innovative fiction was all about itself, or about not being about anything else; and that being the case there was little point in descending to the specifics of such fiction—it was essentially all the same. This situation was consolidated by criticism's appropriation of the discourse of postmodernism, which imposed a specious uniformity upon its referents even as it affirmed their diversity. By various strategies of transcendence it incorporated heterogeneity as a quality of postmodern fiction; at the same time its abstractions were severed from their sources by a self-referentiality that collapsed meta-levels into theoretical immanence, rendering the critical discourse itself both autonomous and paradoxical. For opponents of innovative fiction this could only confirm its reputation as the formalistic antithesis to realism's preoccupation with matters of substance. Such a view is refuted by the fictions I have discussed here, which treat formal innovation in a way far from antithetical to substantial concerns; instead, they make it a vital agent of the *articulation* of those concerns.

Ultimately, the inadequacy of so much criticism to the enterprise of innovative fiction derives from our tendency to dichotomize form and substance: as a result of this opposition, critical discourse that attends to one term almost always neglects the other. Innovative fiction indubitably presents itself most immediately to the critic as *formally* interesting, and consequently elicits attention to its formal characteristics. But whereas this formal innovation ought to be conceived of as the articulation of the work's substance, the largely substance-oriented approach of literary criticism often results in form being conceived of as *itself* that substance. Critics know how to talk about the substance of a work and make it sound like literature; discussing form, they are caught between the work's tendency to revert to the status of a dumb object, and a compensatory manoeuvre that treats its formal characteristics as themselves the substantial focus of the work. Hence innovative fiction is either about itself, or it is significant only in its formal peculiarity—that is to say, as an aesthetic exercise or "experiment." Yet to say that form is the articulation of substance, that substance is that which is articulated in form, that the two, in short, are inseparable, is only to express a critical commonplace that receives universal lip-service. The problem, then, is in the terminology—it is very difficult to distinguish form and substance as the complementary *aspects* of a work that they are, without being led on to treat them as the independent *qualities* they are not and cannot be. The form/substance distinction is prone to transference from the conceptual perspective of the critic to the innate nature of the fiction. Yet there is no obvious term that expresses these two aspects of fiction in their unity, providing the means to articulate the implication of each in the other. It is in this context that I have attempted to apply the term "argument."

An argument may be perceived in two distinct but complementary ways, according to the position from which it is viewed. It might be regarded from within its frame of reference, in which case its substantial attributes would dominate; or it might be seen from an external perspective, which would give priority to its formal attributes. Treating the formal and substantial aspects of a work in this way, as the products of an exterior or interior perspective upon it, helps to clarify the central problem of the critical debate about innovative fiction: the failure to appreciate its use of form to generate alternative modes of engagement with reality. Attention to the substance of a work places the reader within it, so that a division is established between the situation of the reader in the text and in the world, and the relation between text and reality is as readily assimilated as is the unity of this bifurcated reader. But attention to the form of a work places the reader outside it, relocating this division between the reader and the text, and collapsing text and reality into a monistic, and therefore nonreferential, equivalence. The latter perspective has held sway in the criticism of innovative fiction, and this fiction has accordingly been derided, and celebrated, for an autonomy or object-status that is in fact a product of the sort of attention brought to it.

The concept of the argument of fiction provides a means of relocating the site of a fiction's aboutness. It is not to be found in its substance, nor in its form, but in the formal achievement of its substance; as such it is inextricable from process—the process of writing and the process of reading. The argument of a novel is something that is worked through. It is not an abstract, but ubiquitous, and the meanings of criticism must always retain an awareness that they are the products of a reading—that their unity and closure are hypothetical. The criticism of fiction is in the first instance less "an interpretation" than a report. It needs to attend to the argument as a multidimensional effect of the reading, invested with emotional, aesthetic and rational attributes. Above all it needs to recognize that the argument of a novel constitutes a means of literary engagement beyond mimesis: it is not a representational model, but a discursive one. Among other things, such a recognition immediately releases the criticism of innovative fiction from the misconceived dogma of its autonomy.

Of course it follows that the opposition between innovative and realist fictions is misleading, and that the concept of the argument of fiction applies to both. I have insisted upon the affective qualities of argument because, by abandoning realism, innovative fiction is so often perceived to have forfeited emotional involvement. These novels do offer emotional involvement: it is a direct consequence of the reader's investment in the argument. And I would suggest that this is also the way it works in realist fiction: that the reader's empathy with certain characters is not dependent upon their appearance as real people in real situations but upon their function as the vehicles of certain affective dimensions of the argument. The characters, in other words, are always part of the fiction—just as its content or substance is always to be understood as formed.

The difference between innovative fiction and realism, then, is one of means rather than ends. Innovative fiction is not exclusively preoccupied with form, any more than realism is unmediated content. Form, it is true, has been relatively underplayed in the realist tradition, its exploration inhibited by the mimetic imperative to veil artifice with convention. Nevertheless, content is not literature until it is formed; it is not the material in itself that counts, but the argument of its formulation. Innovative fiction is the attempt to extend the scope of the novel by giving the creative imagination access to the full potential of its means. Its exploration of formal possibilities is not to be viewed and judged as a rejuvenation of form for its own sake, but as a rejuvenation of the *argument* of fiction.

Notes

PREFACE

1. *OED,* senses 3a, b, c; sense 4. This last sense coincides with "argumentation," a semantic overlap that originates in the partially interchangeable Latin terms "argumentum" and "argumentatio."

1 THE IDEA OF INNOVATIVE FICTION

1. Kim Herzinger, "Introduction: On the New Fiction," *Mississippi Review* 40–41 (1985): 8.
2. John Barth, "A Few Words About Minimalism," *New York Times Book Review,* Dec. 28, 1986: 25.
3. See Tony Tanner, *City of Words: American Fiction 1950–70* (London: Jonathan Cape, 1971); Mas'ud Zavarzadeh, *The Mythopoeic Reality: The Postwar American Nonfiction Novel* (Urbana: University of Illinois Press, 1976); Raymond Olderman, *Beyond the Wasteland: A Study of the American Novel in the Nineteen-Sixties* (New Haven: Yale University Press, 1972).
4. John Barth, "The Literature of Exhaustion," *Atlantic,* Aug. 1967: 29.
5. Ibid., 31.
6. Susan Sontag, *Against Interpretation* (New York: Noonday, 1966), 13, 14.
7. William Gass, *Fiction and the Figures of Life* (Boston: Nonpareil, 1971), 25.
8. Ibid., 17.
9. Philip Stevick, "Metaphors for the Novel," *TriQuarterly* 30 (1974); rpt. in *Alternative Pleasures: Postrealist Fiction and the Tradition* (Urbana: University of Illinois Press, 1981), 12.
10. Ibid., 45.
11. Ibid., 45.
12. Leslie Fiedler, "Cross the Border—Close the Gap," 1969; rpt. in *The Collected Essays of Leslie Fiedler,* 2 vols. (New York: Stein and Day, 1971), 2: 461–85.

13. Jacques Derrida, "Structure, Sign and Play in the Discourse of the Human Sciences," *The Languages of Criticism and the Sciences of Man: The Structuralist Controversy,* ed. Richard Macksey and Eugenio Donato, proc. of an international symposium, Oct. 18–21, 1966 (Baltimore: Johns Hopkins University Press, 1970); rpt. in *Writing and Difference,* trans. Alan Bass (London: Routledge, 1978), 279.

14. Ibid., 292.

15. Ibid., 293.

16. William Gass, "Representation and the War for Reality," *Salmagundi* 55 (1982): 101.

17. Ibid., 87–8.

18. Ronald Sukenick, *In Form: Digressions on the Act of Fiction* (Carbondale: Southern Illinois University Press, 1985), 237.

19. Roland Barthes, "To Write: An Intransitive Verb?" *The Languages of Criticism,* ed. Macksey, 144.

20. Ibid., 142.

21. Roland Barthes, *Critical Essays,* trans. Richard Howard (Evanston: Northwestern University Press, 1972), 144–5.

22. Jerome Klinkowitz, *Literary Disruptions: The Making of a Post-Contemporary American Fiction* (Urbana: University of Illinois Press, 1975), 175.

23. Jerome Klinkowitz, *The Self-Apparent Word: Fiction as Language/Language as Fiction* (Carbondale: Southern Illinois University Press, 1984), 59.

24. Ronald Sukenick, "The New Tradition," *Partisan Review* 39 (1972): 587–8.

25. Raymond Federman, "Surfiction—Four Propositions in Form of an Introduction," *Surfiction: Fiction Now . . . and Tomorrow,* ed. Federman (Chicago: Swallow, 1975), 8.

26. Ronald Sukenick, "Thirteen Digressions," *Partisan Review* 43 (1973); rpt. in *In Form,* 31.

27. John Gardner, *On Moral Fiction* (New York: Basic, 1978); Gerald Graff, *Literature Against Itself: Literary Ideas in Modern Society* (Chicago: University of Chicago Press, 1979); John Aldridge, *The American Novel and the Way We Live Now* (Oxford: Oxford University Press, 1983); Charles Newman, *The Post-Modern Aura: The Act of Fiction in an Age of Inflation* (Evanston: Northwestern University Press, 1985).

28. Graff, *Literature Against Itself,* 223.

29. Ibid., 239.

30. Jean Baudrillard, *In the Shadow of the Silent Majorities, or, The End of the Social, and Other Essays,* trans. Paul Foss, John Johnston and Paul Patton (New York: Semiotext(e), 1983), 102.

31. Jean Baudrillard, "On Nihilism," *On The Beach* 6 (Spring 1984); quoted in *Jean Baudrillard: From Marxism to Postmodernism and Beyond,* by Douglas Kellner (Cambridge: Polity, 1989), 119.

32. Jean Baudrillard, "The Precession of Simulacra," *Simulations,* trans. Paul Foss, Paul Patton and Philip Bleitchman (New York: Semiotext(e), 1983), 10.

33. "A Debate: William Gass and John Gardner," *Anything Can Happen: Interviews with Contemporary American Novelists,* ed. Tom LeClair and Larry McCaffery (Urbana: University of Illinois Press, 1983), 24.
34. Gardner, *On Moral Fiction,* 114.
35. John Barth, "The Literature of Replenishment: Postmodernist Fiction," *Atlantic,* Jan. 1980: 70.
36. Newman, *The Post-Modern Aura,* 202.
37. Jerome Klinkowitz, "Experimental Realism in Recent American Painting and Fiction," *Representation and Performance in Postmodern Fiction,* ed. Maurice Couturier, proc. of the Nice Conference on Postmodern Fiction, Apr. 1982 (Montpellier: Université Paul Valéry, 1983), 155.
38. Ibid., 162.
39. Alan Wilde, *Middle Grounds: Studies in Contemporary American Fiction* (Philadelphia: University of Pennsylvania Press, 1987), 4.
40. Ibid., 24.
41. Ibid., 25.
42. Ibid., 34.
43. John Hawkes, interview, *Wisconsin Studies in Contemporary Literature* 6 (Summer 1965): 149.
44. Ibid., 149.
45. Ibid., 143.
46. William Burroughs, "The Cut Up Method," *The Moderns: An Anthology of New Writing in America,* ed. LeRoi Jones (London: MacGibbon & Kee, 1965), 346.
47. William Burroughs, *The Job: Interviews with William S. Burroughs,* with Daniel Odier (London: Jonathan Cape, 1970), 12.
48. Susan Sontag, interview, *The New Fiction: Interviews with Innovative American Writers,* ed. Joe David Bellamy (Urbana: University of Illinois Press, 1974), 120.
49. Sontag, *Against Interpretation,* 35.
50. Thomas Pynchon, *The Crying of Lot 49* (1966; London: Pan, 1979), 89.
51. Charles Caramello, "Flushing Out 'The Voice in the Closet,' " *SubStance* 20 (1978); rpt. in *Silverless Mirrors: Book, Self & Postmodern American Fiction* (Tallahassee: University Presses of Florida, 1983), 132. Federman himself quotes the phrase in *The Twofold Vibration.*
52. Raymond Federman, *The Twofold Vibration* (Bloomington: Indiana University Press, 1982), 1.
53. Richard Brautigan, *Trout Fishing in America* (New York: Dell, 1967), 78.
54. Donald Barthelme, "After Joyce," *Location* 2 (1964): 13.
55. Donald Barthelme, "Not-Knowing," *Georgia Review* 39 (1985): 521.
56. Barthelme, "After Joyce," 14.
57. Barthelme, "Not-Knowing," 522.
58. Ibid.
59. Ibid., 512.

60. Fredric Jameson, "The Politics of Theory: Ideological Positions in the Post-modernism Debate," *New German Critique* 33 (1984); rpt. in *The Ideologies of Theory: Essays 1971–1986*, 2 vols. (London: Routledge, 1988), 2: 103–14.

61. Brian McHale, *Postmodernist Fiction* (London: Methuen, 1987).

62. Ibid., 232.

63. Alan Wilde, *Horizons of Assent: Modernism, Postmodernism and the Ironic Imagination* (Baltimore: Johns Hopkins University Press, 1981), 10.

64. Charles Russell, *Poets, Prophets and Revolutionaries: The Literary Avant-Garde From Rimbaud Through Postmodernism* (New York: Oxford University Press, 1985), 253.

65. Ibid., 246.

66. Jean-François Lyotard, *The Postmodern Condition: A Report on Knowledge*, trans. Geoff Bennington and Brian Massumi (Manchester: Manchester University Press, 1984), xxiii.

67. Jean-François Lyotard, "Answering the Question: What Is Postmodernism?" *Innovation/Renovation*, ed. Hassan; rpt. as appendix to *The Postmodern Condition*, 79.

68. Ibid., 81.

69. Jean-François Lyotard, *Just Gaming*, trans. Wlad Godzich (Manchester: Manchester University Press, 1985), 100.

70. Fredric Jameson, "Postmodernism and Consumer Society," *Postmodern Culture*, ed. Hal Foster (London: Pluto, 1985), 125.

71. Fredric Jameson, *Postmodernism, or, The Cultural Logic of Late Capitalism* (London: Verso, 1991), 418.

72. Ibid., x.

73. Ibid., xxii.

74. Graff, *Literature Against Itself*, 225.

75. Ihab Hassan, *The Dismemberment of Orpheus: Toward a Postmodern Literature*, 2nd ed. (Madison: University of Wisconsin Press, 1982), 263.

76. Susan Suleiman, "Naming and Difference: Reflections on 'Modernism versus Postmodernism' in Literature," *Approaching Postmodernism*, ed. Douwe Fokkema and Hans Bertens (Amsterdam: John Benjamins, 1986), 261–2.

77. Hassan, *The Dismemberment of Orpheus*, 269.

78. Linda Hutcheon, "Beginning to Theorize Postmodernism," *Textual Practice* 1 (1987): 17.

79. Ibid., 19.

80. Ibid.

81. Lyotard, *The Postmodern Condition*, 79; italics added.

82. Ibid., 76.

83. Linda Hutcheon, *Narcissistic Narrative: The Metafictional Paradox* (London: Methuen, 1984), 2.

84. Larry McCaffery, "The Art of Metafiction: William Gass's *Willie Masters' Lonesome Wife*," *Critique* 18 (1976): 21.

85. William Gass, *Willie Masters' Lonesome Wife*, *TriQuarterly Supplement No. 2* (Evanston: Northwestern University Press, 1968); rpt. (Lisle: Dalkey Archive,

1989). The Dalkey Archive edition homogenizes the paper. Neither is paginated.

86. Sarah Lauzen, "Notes on Metafiction: Every Essay Has a Title," *Postmodern Fiction: A Bio-Bibliographical Guide,* ed. Larry McCaffery (New York: Greenwood, 1986), 98, 105.

87. Thomas LeClair, "William Gaddis, *JR,* and the Art of Excess," *Modern Fiction Studies* 27 (1981–2): 587–600.

88. Lauzen, "Notes on Metafiction," 94.

89. Patricia Waugh, *Metafiction: The Theory and Practice of Self-Conscious Fiction* (London: Methuen, 1984), 2. Italics added.

90. Larry McCaffery, *The Metafictional Muse: The Works of Robert Coover, Donald Barthelme, and William H. Gass* (Pittsburgh: University of Pittsburgh Press, 1982), 6.

91. John Barth, *Lost in the Funhouse* (1968; New York: Doubleday, 1988), 1–2. Subsequent references in the text are to this edition.

2 HOW TO SUCCEED: DONALD BARTHELME'S *THE DEAD FATHER*

1. Donald Barthelme, *Snow White* (1967; New York: Atheneum, 1987), 82–3. Subsequent references in the text are to this edition.

2. Richard Schickel, "Freaked Out on Barthelme," *New York Times Magazine,* Aug. 16, 1970: 15.

3. Donald Barthelme, interview, *Anything Can Happen: Interviews with Contemporary American Novelists,* ed. Tom LeClair and Larry McCaffery (Urbana: University of Illinois Press, 1983), 40–41.

4. Donald Barthelme, "Donald Barthelme: The Art of Fiction LXVI," *Paris Review* 23 (1981): 199.

5. Maureen Howard, "Recent Novels: A Backward Glance," *Yale Review* 65 (1976): 408.

6. Roger Shattuck, "*The Dead Father,*" *New York Times Book Review,* Nov. 9, 1975: 50.

7. Howard, "Recent Novels: A Backward Glance," 408.

8. Barthelme, "The Art of Fiction LXVI," 199.

9. Richard Todd, "Daddy, You're perfectly swell!" *Atlantic,* Dec. 1975: 112.

10. Barthelme, interview, *Anything Can Happen,* 41.

11. Barthelme, "The Art of Fiction LXVI," 201.

12. Donald Barthelme, *Unspeakable Practices, Unnatural Acts* (New York: Farrar, 1968); rpt. in *Sixty Stories* (New York: Dutton, 1982), 53–8.

13. Donald Barthelme, *The Dead Father* (London: Routledge, 1977), 3. All subsequent references in the text are to this edition.

14. Donald Barthelme, *Come Back, Dr. Caligari* (Boston: Little, Brown, 1964), 171–83.

15. Barthelme, "The Art of Fiction LXVI," 207–8.

16. Donald Barthelme, *Sadness* (New York: Farrar, 1972); rpt. in *Forty Stories* (London: Secker, 1988), 130–40.
17. Barthelme, "The Art of Fiction LXVI," 190, 189.
18. Donald Barthelme, *Great Days* (London: Routledge, 1979), 21–38.
19. Barthelme, "The Art of Fiction LXVI," 197.

3 "A MAN'S STORY IS HIS GRIS-GRIS": CULTURAL
SLAVERY, LITERARY EMANCIPATION AND
ISHMAEL REED'S *FLIGHT TO CANADA*

1. Addison Gayle, Jr., ed., *The Black Aesthetic* (Garden City: Doubleday, 1971).
2. Ishmael Reed, "When State Magicians Fail: An Interview with Ishmael Reed," *Journal of Black Poetry* 1 (1969): 75.
3. Ishmael Reed, *Yellow Back Radio Broke-Down* (1969; New York: Atheneum, 1988), 36.
4. Henry Louis Gates, Jr., "The 'Blackness of Blackness': A Critique of the Sign and the Signifying Monkey," *Critical Enquiry* 9 (1983): 701.
5. Ishmael Reed, interview, *The New Fiction: Interviews with Innovative American Writers,* ed. Joe David Bellamy (Urbana: University of Illinois Press, 1974), 133.
6. Ishmael Reed, *Shrovetide in Old New Orleans* (Garden City: Doubleday, 1978), 233.
7. Ishmael Reed, *Cab Calloway Stands In For The Moon* (Flint: Bamberger, 1986); published as "D Hexorcism of Noxon D Awful," in *19 Necromancers from Now,* ed. Reed (New York: Doubleday, 1970).
8. Reed, *Shrovetide in Old New Orleans,* 133.
9. Ibid., 232–3.
10. W. C. Bamberger, "The Waxing and Waning of Cab Calloway," *Review of Contemporary Fiction* 4 (1984): 204.
11. Ishmael Reed, *Mumbo Jumbo* (1972; New York: Atheneum, 1988), 160.
12. Ishmael Reed, *Flight to Canada* (New York: Random House, 1976), 11. All subsequent references in the text are to this edition.
13. Henry Louis Gates, Jr., rev. of *Flight to Canada, Journal of Negro History* 63 (1978): 78.
14. Ishmael Reed, interview, *Interviews with Black Writers,* ed. John O'Brien (New York: Liveright, 1973), 174.
15. Reed, interview, *The New Fiction,* 138.
16. Ishmael Reed, "An Interview with Ishmael Reed," *Iowa Review* 13 (1982): 129.
17. Reed, *Shrovetide in Old New Orleans,* 228–9.
18. Ishmael Reed, "An Interview with Ishmael Reed," *Review of Contemporary Fiction* 4 (1984): 179.
19. Ibid., 186.

20. Gates, rev. of *Flight to Canada,* 80.

21. Reed, *Mumbo Jumbo,* 69.

22. Reed, *Shrovetide in Old New Orleans,* 210.

23. Earlier in the novel, the "Nebraska Tracers" who attempt to repossess the fugitive Quickskill consider appropriating his poem (that is, disenfranchising him of his culture) and evade questions of copyright by citing the precedent of the Dredd Scott case: "he doesn't come within the framework of Anglo-Saxon law. Justice Taney said that a slave has no rights that a white man is bound to respect" (63).

24. Reed was editor of *19 Necromancers from Now* (1970); co-founded Yardbird Publishing Co. (1971); produced five volumes of the *Yardbird Reader* (1972–6); co-founded Reed, Cannon & Johnson Communications (1973); established the Before Columbus Foundation (1976); served as editor-in-chief of *Y'Bird* magazine (1978–80); and co-founded *Quilt* (1980).

4 NARRATIVE INSCRIPTION, HISTORY AND THE READER IN ROBERT COOVER'S *THE PUBLIC BURNING*

1. Robert Coover, interview, *Anything Can Happen: Interviews with Contemporary American Novelists,* ed. Tom LeClair and Larry McCaffery (Urbana: University of Illinois Press, 1983), 77.

2. Robert Coover, *The Public Burning* (New York: Viking, 1977), 407. All subsequent references in the text are to this edition.

3. Robert Coover, rev. of *The Implosion Conspiracy,* by Louis Nizer, *New York Times Book Review,* Feb. 11, 1973: 5.

4. "Rosenberg Son Gets Word of Fate on TV," *The New York Times,* June 20, 1953: 6.

5. Richard Andersen, *Robert Coover* (Boston: G. K. Hall, 1981), 124.

6. Robert Coover, quoted in Thomas Alden Bass, "An Encounter with Robert Coover," *Antioch Review* 40 (1982): 297.

7. Coover, interview, *Anything Can Happen,* 66.

8. Ibid., 74.

9. David Estes, "American Folk Laughter in Robert Coover's *The Public Burning,*" *Contemporary Literature* 28 (1987): 239–56.

10. Thomas R. Edwards, "Real People, Mythic History," rev. of *The Public Burning, New York Times Book Review,* Aug. 14, 1977: 9.

11. Emile Durkheim, *The Elementary Forms of the Religious Life,* trans. Joseph Ward Swain (London: George Allen & Unwin, n.d. [1915]), 210.

12. Mikhail Bakhtin, *Rabelais and His World,* trans. Hélène Iswolsky (Bloomington: Indiana University Press, 1984), 11–12.

13. Robert Coover, "An Interview with Robert Coover," *Critique* 11 (1969): 28.

14. Bakhtin, *Rabelais and His World*, 67, 66.
15. Larry McCaffery, *The Metafictional Muse: The Works of Robert Coover, Donald Barthelme and William H. Gass* (Pittsburgh: University of Pittsburgh Press, 1982), 89.
16. Coover, interview, *Anything Can Happen*, 68.
17. Ibid., 74.

5 "ONE'S IMAGE OF ONESELF": STRUCTURED IDENTITY IN WALTER ABISH'S *HOW GERMAN IS IT*

1. Walter Abish, quoted in Jerome Klinkowitz, *The Life of Fiction* (Urbana: University of Illinois Press, 1977), 68.
2. Walter Abish, *How German Is It* (New York: New Directions, 1980; London: Faber, 1983), 53. All subsequent references in the text are to this edition.
3. Abish, quoted in Klinkowitz, *The Life of Fiction*, 67.
4. Walter Abish, "The Writer-To-Be: An Impression of Living," *SubStance* 27 (1980): 109.
5. Walter Abish, quoted in Christopher Butler, "Scepticism and Experimental Fiction," *Essays in Criticism* 36 (1986): 64.
6. Edward Marcotte, "Intersticed Prose," *Chicago Review* 26 (1975): 33.
7. Michael Hofmann, rev. of *How German Is It*, *Times Literary Supplement*, Apr. 2, 1982: 395.
8. Douglas Messerli, "The Role of Voice in NonModernist Fiction," *Contemporary Literature* 25 (1984): 281–304.
9. Ibid., 300.
10. Richard Martin, "Walter Abish's Fictions: Perfect Unfamiliarity, Familiar Imperfections," *Journal of American Studies* 17 (1983): 238.
11. Abish, quoted in Klinkowitz, *The Life of Fiction*, 68.
12. Walter Abish, "The English Garden," *In the Future Perfect* (1977; London: Faber, 1984).
13. Abish, quoted in Klinkowitz, *The Life of Fiction*, 69.
14. Roland Barthes, *Mythologies*, trans. Annette Lavers (1970; London: Paladin, 1973), 9.
15. Ibid., 142.
16. Walter Abish, "On Aspects of the Familiar World as Perceived in Everyday Life and Literature," paper read at the Second International Conference on Innovation/Renovation in Contemporary Culture, Milwaukee 1981; cited in Martin, "Walter Abish's Fictions," 234.
17. Abish, quoted in Klinkowitz, *The Life of Fiction*, 63.
18. Walter Abish, interview, *Alive and Writing*, ed. Larry McCaffery and Sinda Gregory (University of Illinois Press, 1987), 16.
19. Abish, quoted in Martin, "Walter Abish's Fictions," 241.

6 THE QUEST FOR LOVE AND THE WRITING OF FEMALE DESIRE IN KATHY ACKER'S *DON QUIXOTE*

1. Bonnie Zimmerman, "Feminist Fiction and the Postmodern Challenge," *Postmodern Fiction: A Bio-Bibliographical Guide,* ed. Larry McCaffery (New York: Greenwood, 1986), 186.

2. Kathy Acker, interview, "In the Tradition of Cervantes, Sort Of," *New York Times Book Review,* Nov. 30, 1986: 10.

3. Kathy Acker, *Don Quixote* (London: Grafton, 1986), 109. All subsequent references in the text are to this edition.

4. Miguel de Cervantes Saavedra, *Don Quixote,* trans. J. M. Cohen (Harmondsworth: Penguin, 1950), part II, chap. 23.

5. Acker, interview, "In the Tradition of Cervantes, Sort Of," 10.

6. Ibid., 10.

7. Kathy Acker, interview, "A Radical American Abroad," *Drama* 160 (1986): 17.

8. Acker, interview, "In the Tradition of Cervantes, Sort Of," 10.

9. Acker, interview, "A Radical American Abroad," 17.

10. Ann Haverly, "In the (K)night-time," rev. of *Don Quixote, Times Literary Supplement,* May 23, 1986: 554.

11. Kathy Acker, "Models of Our Present," *Artforum,* Feb. 1984: 64.

12. Ibid., 64.

13. Julia Kristeva, *Powers of Horror: An Essay on Abjection,* trans. Leon S. Roudiez (New York: Columbia University Press, 1982), 5.

14. Luce Irigaray, *This Sex Which Is Not One,* trans. Catherine Porter (New York: Cornell University Press, 1985).

15. Kathy Acker, introduction, *Boxcar Bertha: An Autobiography,* as told to Dr. Ben L. Reitman (New York: Amok, 1988), x–xi.

16. Cindy Patton, "Post-Punk Feminism," *Women's Review of Books* 1 (1984); quoted in Glenn A. Harper, "The Subversive Power of Sexual Difference in the Work of Kathy Acker," *SubStance* 16 (1987): 48.

17. Acker, interview, "A Radical American Abroad," 17.

18. Patton, "Post-Punk Feminism," 17.

19. Irigaray, *This Sex Which Is Not One,* 28.

20. Acker, interview, "A Radical American Abroad," 17.

21. Tom LeClair, "The Lord of La Mancha and Her Abortion," rev. of *Don Quixote, New York Times Book Review,* Nov. 30, 1986: 10.

22. David Van Leer, "Punko Panza," rev. of *Don Quixote, New Republic,* May 4, 1987: 40.

23. Danny Karlin, "Antinomian Chic," rev. of *Empire of the Senseless* and "Russian Constructivism" (extract from *Don Quixote*), *London Review of Books,* June 2, 1988: 10.

24. Acker, "Models of Our Present," 64.

Index

Abish, Walter, 10, 162; *Alphabetical Africa,* 111–12, 117, 121; and defamiliarization, 111–12, 121; *In The Future Perfect,* 111; *Minds Meet,* 111; "On Aspects of the Familiar World as Perceived in Everyday Life and Literature," 124; "The English Garden," 120; "The Writer-To-Be: An Impression of Living," 112–13

Abish, Walter, *How German Is It:* explanatory structures in, 112–14, 132–3; and the familiar, 116, 124–6; and the new Germany, 118–19, 126–9, 132–3; novelist-protagonist in, 112–13, 120; order in, 126–7; self-consciousness of, 114–17, 133; structured identity in, 118–21, 129–32

Acker, Kathy, ix, 162; *Blood and Guts in High School,* 135, 142; *Empire of the Senseless,* 155; and feminism, 147–9; *Great Expectations,* 142; *The Childlike Life of the Black Tarantula,* 142

Acker, Kathy, *Don Quixote:* asociality of, 140–2; and Cervantes, 136–8; desire and control in, 143–7, 149–51; and emotional nihilism, 151–2; language and community in, 157–60; and narrative, 138–40, 152–3; and plagiarism, 136, 153–5; pornography

in, 146–7; self and text in, 155–7

Addison, Joseph, xi

Aldridge, John, 12

Andersen, Richard, 89–90

Apple, Max, 16, 162

argument, viii, x–xi, 18, 42, 164–6, 167

Aristotle, 17

Arnold, June, 135

autonomy, viii, 3–5, 35–7, 42, 163, 165

avant-garde, x, 30, 34

Baker, Houston, 66

Bakhtin, Mikhail, 95, 96–7

Baraka, Imamu Amiri, 66, 83

Barth, John, 1, 3, 15, 32, 162; *Lost in the Funhouse,* 40–2

Barthelme, Donald, ix, 16, 32, 161; "A Shower of Gold," 49; "After Joyce," 24–5; *Great Days,* 50, 56; "Not-Knowing," 24–6; *Snow White,* 43; "The Balloon," 47; "The Flight of the Pigeons from the Palace," 50; "The New Music," 51

Barthelme, Donald, *The Dead Father:* as allegory, 46–7, 52; diagrams in, 53; dialogues in, 54–7; and involvement, 62–3; language in, 51–7; "Manual for Sons," 61–2; narrative and authority in, 57–9; and the new, 50–1; and the old order, 47–

CAMBRIDGE STUDIES IN AMERICAN LITERATURE AND CULTURE

Continued from the front of the book

The following titles are out of print:

For EU product safety concerns, contact us at Calle de José Abascal, 56–1°, 28003 Madrid, Spain or eugpsr@cambridge.org.

www.ingramcontent.com/pod-product-compliance
Ingram Content Group UK Ltd.
Pitfield, Milton Keynes, MK11 3LW, UK
UKHW010046140625
459647UK00012BB/1650